The Point of Convergence: A Path to Understanding Conflict Resolution

TABLE OF CONTENTS

The Point of Convergence: A Path to Understanding Conflict Resolution

Book edited by Ms. Chris Rogers

Cover design by Rick Boggan of Rick Boggan Graphic Design

INTRODUCTION

While the clenched fist prevents loss of that it clutches, it cannot receive that which might become available. (Milt Thomas)

In the early years of this new century, mediation was everyone's favorite buzz word. The subject of mediation was very much in vogue due to books written by Christopher W. Moore, William Ury, Jack Gordon, and others. During this period, hyperbole was the order of the day.

It was common to read things like "growth will get to social and behavioral proportions where everyone will be doing it and conflict management processes and systems will become essential to organizational life...." The reality is much different, and for good reasons.

It is true that a number of well-known companies such as General Electric, Prudential, Johnson & Johnson, and others recognized the value of mediation as a tool for solving conflict. These companies hired and trained employees to arbitrate, mediate, and act as ombudsmen within their organizations.

For the broader business community the idea of conflict resolution outside the legal arena was a tougher obstacle to overcome, and to some degree it still is.

The main reason is, in many situations, it is hard to quantify the value before engaging in the process.

The Point of Convergence: A Path to Understanding Conflict Resolution

While alternative dispute processes are becoming more widely accepted, many still misunderstand what they are and how these processes function.

For example, it still catches many by surprise when they discover that more than half of all voluntary resignations relate directly to unresolved conflict. The percentage is substantially higher when it involves employees who are forced to leave the company they work for. And those that do know this still struggle to find solutions to this primary driver of employee turnover.

This book is the product of more than 40 years of experience with conflict and the challenges of getting the party(s) to agree on a course of action. One of the earliest lessons I learned is that no formula exists where variables get plugged in according to a set of rules and, bingo, you reach agreement.

What one quickly learns is that there are processes that work, and techniques that work, and methods of inquiry that work. The challenge for anyone taking on a conflict resolution challenge is combining these into workable strategies to advance a successful outcome.

One also learns that each of these must be configured to the challenges of a specific conflict, and the environment where that conflict achieved its "critical mass".

One quickly learns the efforts to understand the true reasons for the conflict require both time and resources.

This fact creates an additional obstacle to creating the right strategy for success.

The Point of Convergence: A Path to Understanding Conflict Resolution

Behavior drives conflict. This is a theme that I touch on at various points along the way in this book. In an earlier book I wrote on ethics and integrity and I touched on the influences on that subject by St. Thomas Aquinas. He had an equally long lasting impact on the notion of conflict.

While his <u>Summa Theologiae</u> focuses on whether or not war is ever just, his writings have impacted the whole idea of conflict for more than 700 years.

From his writings and the experience learned over those centuries, we know that many conflicts are just because the motives that underlie these conflicts is just or righteous, especially when they don't involve weapons of war. Our own nation's history gives us examples where the threat of war was enough to prevent war.

We know conflict in many contexts clarifies things, makes things better, and advances understanding. In Thomas Aquinas's theological arguments, he defined the virtue of justice that echoes through our everyday lives, and surprisingly, is of more than passing importance in understanding conflict inside the business environment.

For lack of a better term, this landmark thesis, took the search for truth out of the theological sphere, and placed it in the world of logic and reason.

And solving conflicts in the business world is about determining the facts, and only after that is accomplished, determining what they mean, and how they can be applied.

One of those truths is that all organizations have structures where authority and power are different based on where you work, and the value that you bring to that organization. Because of this, the balance of power is never equal, and that creates tensions that are never fully resolved.

In every such structure a point exists, often more than one, where a gap is created. It may exist because it developed in the organization over time through a lack of diligence, or it may form because of how people around this gap think and behave.

This gap is a nexus, a Point of Convergence, which acts much like a whirlpool, and the whirlpool inside these gaps is created by behaviors and actions that interact like currents of water react to each other. The interactions of behaviors inside the point of convergence, like a whirlpool, creates an energy that pulls other behaviors into the center.

In every organization people make decisions based on expediency. Many of these decisions, unsurprisingly, follow the path of least resistance, and generate behaviors that support and rationalize these decisions. It is here where the counter-currents begin to form.

These expediency driven behaviors pull on other behaviors. They converge into the center, and, like water currents, thrust and pull at each other, and are scattered randomly. This center creates energy that drives behaviors which can cause unsafe acts, unethical acts, and the acts that create conflict.

The behaviors that flow from these points of convergence is the principle focus of this book. As noted above, I will review the other behaviors that flow from these gaps as a means of establishing a fuller context, but the primary focus of this book is to examine why conflict is misunderstood, and mismanaged at multiple steps along the way.

As you will discover within the pages of this book, conflict resolution requires that one learn how to use words differently. Clarity in the use of words and phrases will take on new importance.

Unsurprisingly, few people have the natural ability, skills, and self-control to guide others through a conflict. Most of us need to learn these skills, learn the kind of self-discipline, and the patience this process requires. Disagreements, fights, occur for a wide range of reasons; some complex, and some not.

Arguments over access to copiers and computer equipment may appear petty and small minded, but where schedules are demanding and resources are in short supply, people's sense of perspective quickly disappears.

Therefore the problem is not so much, to see what nobody has yet seen, but rather to think concerning that which everybody sees, what nobody has yet thought. (A quote attributed to Arthur Schopenhauer)

This gap exists because decisions are frequently made that do not align with broader plans and strategies, because for many inside an organization, what matters is getting work done. As a result, expediency wins out over how things should be done.

It is only after the train derails that efforts are made to do it better in the future. One of the things illustrated in these pages is how challenging it becomes to align goals and performance once conflict degrades the work environment.

I wish to express my deep appreciation to those of you who decided to spend time within these pages. It is my sincere wish that you find the time you spend here to be both interesting and informative, and I encourage you to reach out to me as provided for at the conclusion of the book to offer comment, or request clarification on any of the things you read.

Chapter 1

Uncovering the Myths

"The past and history are different things" (J.H. Plumb).

The historian J.H. Plum wrote that people do not look at the past as a simple record of what happened. For most, the past explains our purpose and how we fit into the whole. The past provides a window into our origins; dim and imprecise as that view might be and it gives us a process for building a moral framework.

Many have used the past to legitimize government institutions, and a society's legal foundations. The writer, Gil Klein, makes a similar observation when he writes "...most of the American myths are based on historical fact..."

Klein makes the point that Paul Revere did make his famous ride to warn the colonists that British troops had mobilized to seize local militia arsenals, and that Patrick Henry did give a patriotic speech that captured great attention and aroused the surrounding countryside to support General Washington's infant army.

Yet, Paul Revere's ride did not carry the high drama and desperate race against time that is evident in the equally famous poem by Henry Wadsworth Longfellow.

The Point of Convergence: A Path to Understanding Conflict Resolution

No one knows for certain whether Patrick Henry actually said "Give me liberty or give me death," since he spoke before that crowd of people without any notes.

That is the curious blend of fact and fiction that often permeates history. It is also the stuff on which myths are built.

Nevertheless, it is too easy to say that histories are filled with information that is a blend of fact and fiction, and anyone drawing that conclusion would miss the mark. Histories contain facts that are clear – such and such battle fought on these dates and at these locations.

Things are never completely false. The "fiction" part almost always contains a truth that is shaded and colored by those minds that chronicled the initial events.

Our modern understanding of conflict carries this same mishmash of specific knowledge blended with hazy truth – truth that has been shaded and colored by various chroniclers. These blended realities carry forward to today.

History misleads many to believe that future wars will be short, less bloody, or less violent. America's civil war, for example, lasted less than five years, our involvement in WWI was less than three years, and our involvement in WWWII was a little less than four years. The Gulf War of 1991 lasted less than a year.

These "historical" events combine to create the impression that future wars will be of short duration. That a war will be short is a myth that gains traction in spite of evidence to the contrary.

A closer study shows that modern wars, especially civil wars, are as long lasting as other civil wars documented in history books. Yet, this myth has taken hold, and it impacts our present and future decisions.

Myths don't reside only in history books.

Myths permeate our society, our culture, and in many ways they shape how we view the world around us. In an article I wrote not too long ago I refer to myths as peculiar things, and that is because they are a mixture of fact and fiction.

In the normal course of living we learn through experience or education that something is either true or false. We also learn things from stories that are true, and we learn things through stories that turn out not to be true. We may even, without realizing it, interpret facts from stories without giving that interpretation adequate context.

In the not too distant past a myth came crashing into reality with truly comic consequences, and a few near tragedies. From our modern perspective it might seem silly, but for centuries people believed that the other planets in our solar system contained life, and by life I mean sentient beings. Mars, because of its proximity to Earth and the Sun was seen as the planet most likely to hold life similar to ours.

Books by Jules Verne, Edgar Rice Burroughs, and others sustained this myth, and it carried over into our earliest movies. And then on October 30, 1938, *the resonating voice of actor Orson Welles came over radios throughout America with the announcement: "Ladies and gentlemen, we know*

11

now that in the early years of the twentieth century, this world was being watched by intelligences greater than man..."

Unfortunately, many listeners missed the opening statement that the Columbia Broadcasting System was presenting a radio drama of the H.G. Wells book, War of the Worlds.

Listeners who tuned in minutes later, during a dance music segment, caught an even more disturbing message: *"Ladies and gentlemen, we interrupt our program of dance music to bring you a special bulletin from the Intercontinental Radio News... At twenty minutes before eight, central time, Professor Farrell of the Mount Jennings Observatory, Chicago, Illinois, reports observing several explosions of incandescent gas, occurring at regular intervals on the planet Mars. The spectroscope indicates the gas to be hydrogen and moving towards the earth with enormous velocity...."*

The music program continued to be interrupted by news-style reports from Grover's Mill, N.J., where "giant Martian war-machines" had landed. This broadcast, however, marked only the beginning of the myth.

According to a number of wildly exaggerated reports that followed, "Armed with rifles and shotguns, millions of panicked Americans evacuated their homes to flee the Martian invasion dramatized in that pre-Halloween presentation." Other reports stated the numbers of people who were injured or killed during the panic.

Yet, in later years, a national ratings survey reported that a relatively small number of listeners even heard it, due to the program being scheduled against a popular comedy-variety show featuring ventriloquist Edgar Bergen.

Subsequent facts that surfaced tell us that no one was injured and no one died, although one man reported arriving home just in time to stop his terrified wife from swallowing poison.

These facts, however, don't stop people from believing, after all this time, that thousands of American's across the country ran terrorized from their homes while others died trying to escape.

Looking back, it's important to note that real-world events quite likely contributed to the perceived threat.
This was 1938, when Europe was edging toward war with Hitler's Germany, which had just taken over Austria, and was looking to expand to the east into Poland. People were already poised for panic.

This is Where Myths Develop.

We all believe in at least one thing that isn't true. We may not know that what we believe is not true, but among us are some who do know that one or more things they believe is not true, and still choose to continue with that belief.

We all grow up hearing stories from family, relatives, longtime family friends, and from stories in the books and magazines we read. It is no surprise, then, that we take pieces of those stories and shape them into facts that guides some portion of what we think.

What *is* surprising, though, is that myths exist within practical business environments. One might think otherwise, because the business world is all about data, facts, figures, and is driven by goals and objectives.

Yet, myths do exist, and these mythical beliefs make business decisions more complicated than they need to be, and particular myths exist that affect conflict in the workplace.

For example, many believe the following Illusions:

Myth 1. All conflict is bad.

The basic idea here is that workplaces should be free of conflict, and it must be avoided or stopped before everything falls apart. At its core is the notion that conflict equals failure, and we can't have failure in the workplace. Those who hold this view do not realize or cannot conceive that the opposite is true.

Most people find conflict uncomfortable, some even feel threatened by it, and those who feel this way go to great lengths to avoid it or they may look for ways to have others "manage" the conflict for them. The all-conflict-is-bad person sees conflict as interpersonal failure or perceives the parties in a disagreement are behaving in an unprofessional manner.

Interpersonal relationships are complicated. The idea that everything must run smoothly all the time is both unrealistic, and counterproductive. Work environments are complex structures, often unstable under the best of circumstances.

14

Managers and employees who see any conflict as a threat, and then react in a manner that merely stifles the conflict without taking time to understand the underlying factors, will create a much higher level of instability in that work environment.

The notion that all conflict is bad is a myth born and perpetrated by the discomfort it creates. Most often, conflict in a business environments reflects a healthy workplace dynamic, a place where ideas are challenged, shaped, and polished. In that context other people's views and opinions stand balanced against our own perspectives.

The tension that exists during such "give and takes" is crucial to forging better decisions, better relationships, and can actually improve workplace environments.

The majority of disagreements are resolved right where they occur; between and among those individuals most impacted by the situation. Usually, only a small number may need to be mediated by a more senior team member.

An under-appreciated reality is that working teams handle most disagreements through an informal consensus process. Nevertheless, conflicts that fall outside the norm, those requiring intervention or more formal dispute resolution, create a greater impact and color people's perceptions, thus driving this myth.

Myth 2. All conflict can be resolved.

How often have you heard the expression "I know what I know and I believe what I believe"?" Probably too many times to count.

Such rigid positioning reflects a simple truth – that not every disagreement can be solved. People see the world differently, based upon their own history, and they apply their individual perceptions to business as well as personal circumstances.

It is easy to point to conflicts outside the workplace that start as intractable and escalate to hostility.

Wars erupt in various places around the world for a number of reasons, and all wars reflect a failure to resolve disagreements peacefully. It is equally easy to find nonviolent but intractable conflicts outside the workplace that cause long-term damage.

In many work environments, conflicts occur for no other reason than the clash of competing objectives. Engineering departments are reluctant to compromise with operational departments, and operational departments are reluctant to cooperate with those tasked to deliver the product on time.

A point is sometimes reached where you can't change a person's mind, or you won't change your mind, and the issue will not advance further. At that point, if the parties are being responsible, they agree to disagree professionally, courteously, and move on. Not all conflict can be resolved.

The goal in this situation is to move forward anyway, to advance the objective through mutual recognition that it benefits both parties to work amiably in concert to the extent practical.

Myth 3. *Conflict resolution means someone wins and someone loses.*

This is one of the more enduring myths. It is this mindset that leads to many conflicts becoming entrenched, thus creating hostility and suspicion, which adversely impact the workplace in multiple ways. It is this same mindset that often destroys marriages and family relationships, so it should not be taken lightly when a win-lose conflict develops in the workplace.

The give-and-take in human relationships does not mean that everything balances in the end. To borrow briefly from an aspect of game theory, conflict resolution is not a zero-sum process. The gains and losses on one side will never equal the gains and losses on the other side.
As long as the parties to a conflict believe that, they will fail, and their attitude will harm the business relationship; possibly even destroy it.

But – and this is a profoundly important "but", conflict resolution is not about someone winning or losing. Conflicts are resolved by finding a way to compromise, and no agreement is reached without those involved in the disagreement making a decision to look at alternatives.

How many times have you heard someone say; "This is a matter of principle, and I will not compromise"? What that person is really saying is "It's my way or else." Such an intractable attitude reflects a complete and absolute ignorance of what the word "compromise" means. By definition it simply means: to reach an agreement.

The person holding the "my way or else" point of view is clinging to an aspect of the win/loss myth that "compromise means failure," and that by ceding a point or changing your mind, you will lose more than you win.

Confusion and uncertainty also cloud this type of discussion because the word compromise is being changed as a result of attacks on it within our broader culture. The changes to this word are detrimental to effective conflict resolution as I will explain further in Chapter 11, The Culture Paradox.

Myth 4. *Compassion prevents conflict.*

It still surprises me how often people believe that compassion equals empathy, or its cousin, sympathy.

Empathy is being aware of and sensitive to the other party's thoughts and feelings, yet stopping short of investing your own emotions in theirs. Compassion is similar but often includes a desire to help.

A marriage counselor should have compassion for a couple struggling to hold their marriage together. Through compassion, the counselor invests in that couple's struggle. At the same time, that counselor must remain objective enough to counsel the couple toward mutual understanding and consideration.

The Point of Convergence: A Path to Understanding Conflict Resolution

In dismantling the compassion-prevents-conflict myth, it is important to separate truth from fiction, because we need to detach emotion from the issues. Once we do this, it becomes obvious that neither empathy nor compassion prevents conflict.

Empathy, however, is a key component of conflict resolution. Both sides need to understand fully the other person's point of view and to appreciate why that viewpoint is important to that person. Empathy doesn't require that you accept another's point of view, or agree with it, but empathy is the means by which one can see, and possibly understand, the other side.

Compassion, on the other hand, means you are picking sides and sharing what that person is experiencing.

Compassion may lend emotional support to those going through a difficult conflict process, but it doesn't prevent conflict, and to my thinking, has limited value in advancing conflict resolution.

I know beyond any doubt that compassion is key to helping people through difficult times, but only if the one offering compassion has the skill to provide it in the manner needed.

Others in this field may agree or disagree on its role in conflict resolution in a business environment, but in any case, compassion is much more than offering platitudes and adages that sound good.

A number of other myths exist that pertain to conflicts in the workplace, but I think the ones I talk about in this chapter are among the more common.

We spend a great deal of our lives working, and it is no surprise that we bring our understanding of the world around us into the workplace to help us understand how to navigate that aspect of our lives. The stories we rely on to make sense of the world around us, however, have only a limited application in a business environment.

Our Personal Myths Can Become a Driver of Conflict

We create problems for ourselves and others when we fail to recognize that bringing our understanding of the world into the workplace can be and often is a source of conflict.
When faced with conflict, the challenge is to examine our traditional approach, then to ensure we are not adding to the problem by using outdated assumptions.

People often silence themselves, or "agree to disagree" without fully exploring the actual nature of the disagreement, for the sake of protecting a relationship and maintaining connections. But when we avoid certain conversations, and never fully learn how the other person feels about all of the issues, we sometimes end up making assumptions that not only perpetuate but deepen misunderstandings, and that can generate resentment."
(Brené Brown)

20

Other myths about conflict exist, but what I attempted to show with these examples is that relying on one's personal understanding of conflict is often one of the drivers behind disagreements that remain unresolved.

In fact, other drivers exist, in addition to those described above, which may actually create situations that foster conflict.

Already I can hear someone over in the corner whispering, "Do you want a list?" That's just it, anyone can come up with a list, but where do you start?

From my perspective, one of the key drivers, and one that is not given enough attention, is non-compliance with rules.
The levels of departure from established norms in many companies is far wider and more deeply ingrained than their executives or managers may realize. Policies and procedures - the rules – generally exist for good reasons; yet, a surprising number of people are willing to bend the rules for a variety of other reasons.

When someone takes a shortcut, it will inevitably impact someone else in the department or the organization. Modern compliance programs are driven by the requirements of federal and state regulatory agencies to comply with various laws.

These compliance programs are designed, if I may be permitted to use a metaphor, to keep the car from hitting a pothole and potentially damaging the car.

21

The Point of Convergence: A Path to Understanding Conflict Resolution

These same compliance programs, however, often overlook the stones that bruise a heel when that person steps out of the car.

In other words, individuals who deviate from the rules create conflict because they are putting stones in the path of others.

Chapter 2

The Anatomy of Conflict

"There is no greater force of amiability, or ability, than to have strength combined with flexibility." (Ana Claudia Antunes)

A majority of people in a work environment do not understand conflict. They see it play out all around them, but because of myths that abound they have difficulty dealing with the face-to-face reality. As noted in Chapter 1, these vague but persistent myths often prevent conflict resolution.

Add to this problem the mixed results that emerge from efforts to train managers and employees to be more aware of and responsive to workplace conflicts. When someone goes through typical conflict resolution training, he or she is taught what to look for and, generally speaking, has greater confidence and willingness to address a conflict before it gets out of hand.

Yet, those same individuals, when confronted with the task of actually dealing with a workplace conflict are surprised to find the process they're trained for doesn't always work as expected. Not only does the argument or conflict go unresolved, things may actually get worse.

Education Programs and Mixed Results

The Point of Convergence: A Path to Understanding Conflict Resolution

1. Training a group of people inside a company to be mediators or to facilitate employee grievances is time consuming and costly.

2. Adding such factors as promotions, transfers and turnover encourages companies to default to off-the-shelf formulaic approaches or to processes designed around prior experience.

3. No single model fits every situation, and only with experience does someone understand how to adjust a process to accommodate a particular conflict. Conflicts may fall into half a dozen categories, yet no formula for resolving conflict fits neatly into any one category. Each conflict will vary in subtle and important ways that increase the chances for failure when a process or procedure is too prescriptive.

4. In a corporate environment, once a process or procedure is in place, making changes to it is very difficult. Conflicts cannot be defused and negotiated unless the process used helps expose the roots of the quarrel, yet many procedures do not allow the degree of flexibility or "creativity" needed to achieve this.

Modern business language is now held hostage to political correctness and loaded down with words and phrases that can obscure issues. Leaders of an organization may argue strongly that their policies and procedures are free of that taint, yet reality presents the opposite.

Discussions of workplace disagreements is just such an area where modern language impedes efforts to discern the truth;

24

especially when one hears phrases such as "we need to understand how this happened." Yes, understanding the how and why is important, but we hear such a phrase often at the wrong time.

If it is not said as part of a lessons-learned procedure, it comes across as a subtle way of saying "Ok, whose fault is it?" This statement, which sounds reasonable when you first hear it, can actually delay effective conflict resolution. Labeling a person "wrong" immediately creates emotional recoil and sets up roadblocks to resolution.

In a work environment, the arena of conflict management is surrounded by a modern lexicon of buzz words that disguise underlying messages. A common subtext that shows up is "fix it so we don't get sued." This and many similar subtext messages are similar to this and make it difficult to uncover whatever is impacting the workplace or the employees.

Communication within an Organization is Neither Structural nor Linear

Even with training, more than a few individuals never understand or appreciate what's needed to mediate/facilitate a dispute. And by this I don't mean people fail to sit down and write a negotiation plan or some other form of strategy document. I mean their up-front work does not recognize what lies beneath the surface they are about to explore.

To borrow an analogy from botany, you don't have to live in the country to understand that to plant a tree you'll need adequate room for the root system to support that tree over its long life.

Also, you know from practical experience that certain weeds don't sink their roots deep. The roots of weeds stay frequently just below the surface, but run out in many directions for quite a distance.

Removing a mature tree from the ground up is hard work, but a far easier chore when compared to the effort needed to free an area from a pernicious weed. When pulling weeds, you often find yourself repeatedly digging up parts of a root system that you thought had already been removed.

The roots to a conflict combine the worst features of both, in that you have to dig deep, and like a weed, the roots of conflict can spread out and attach themselves where you least expect. I think people understand this, at least on a subjective level, which is one reason they shy away from conflict, preferring to find ways around it.

If you work in a corporate or company environment, you know where you fit on the organization chart. You know many of the people at your level, below you and, to some degree, above you. Those lines on the organization chart make sense to you because you know where you fit.

The various means of communication a company uses will, with few exceptions, follow the lines laid out by the organization chart. When a manager or employee sends or receives information, that individual perceives the information as flowing up or down the communication lines which follow the organizational map.

I take a different view about communication. I argue that much of it is neither structural nor linear. A company may have several methods for disseminating information to employees and may also have several methods for employees to send information up the chain of command. But those channels of communication represent a very small percentage of the information managers and employees receive every day.

Those working inside an organization learn things through a wide array of "sources". In my work and in the articles and books I've written, I talk about what happens when unacceptable behaviors are tolerated. Tolerance for unacceptable behavior never remains localized. It expands to other departments almost like an infectious disease.

How do employees learn about these tolerated behaviors and understand the tacit acceptance of them by management? They don't learn about them through any formal process. Equally important, the knowledge that it is "okay to bend the rules" is more than rumor, and the information gets transmitted differently than through a formal communiqué. What is that mechanism?

Whether we're talking about unsafe acts, unethical acts, or the acts that drive conflict, we're talking about behavior. Information about behavior has a channel of communication that is completely different than most people realize. The metaphor I use in my work is the human nervous system; and sometimes I point to a metabolic pathways chart.

A simple visit to the internet will illustrate what I mean. Flesh, muscle, and sinews react to multiple messages arriving at the same time.

The human nervous system operates with a stunning degree of complexity that defies the ability of most people to describe, yet most people know when it's not working correctly. They sense it, feel it, and react to it.

Taken as a whole, the nervous system is all about interaction. When you understand that information about behaviors travel well established pathways, you begin to understand the relationship between multiple behaviors and conflict.

This book is about the behaviors that drive conflict. But to understand these behaviors, it's important to understand these behaviors are never stand-alone behaviors. Where you find those that drive conflict, you also find those that drive unsafe acts, and unethical acts.

While this book focuses primarily on the subject of conflict resolution, it can't do justice to the subject without understanding where you find one, you find the other two types of behavior, and where all three exist you have the Point of Convergence.

Informal Communication Can Undermine an Organization's Code of Conduct

Once you appreciate how neurological pathways send and receive information, you can more easily understand why traditional lines of communication are largely ineffective when transmitting information about desired behaviors that a company wants to inculcate throughout an organization.

Desired behaviors typically are detailed in the Code of Conduct, with its attendant list of "Do's and Don'ts", and are

28

discussed most often through formal communication methods. Informal discussion of these standards, however, also travels throughout an organization's neural pathways, and more quickly than leaders may realize.

Managers, supervisors, and employees weigh these official messages against what they see going on around them. They assess in real time what they hear or read against what they see, and they react accordingly.

How leaders behave may align with the standards and principles laid down in the Code of Conduct, but the reality is that alignment is elusive. A gap between expectation and execution exists in every company, and a leader's vigilance regarding this gap is what separates truly successful companies from those that are mostly existing on borrowed time.

In my book, *The Battle for Ethics and Integrity in the Workplace: The Leader's Dilemma*, I make the point that some unethical behaviors are more damaging than others.

While any unethical behavior is undesired and, when discovered, needs to be corrected, the reality is more complex.

What many fail to realize is that not all unethical behaviors are the same. While a number of unethical behaviors create an unpleasant work environment, they may not represent an immediate risk.

Others can quickly destabilize a work environment and act as a catalyst for other unethical behaviors. This dichotomy is why some unethical actions are tolerated, while others are not.

Behaviors and their consequences travel the neural pathways of an organization rapidly, and their impact elsewhere can be seen in a surprisingly short amount of time. Too often, a destabilized work environment becomes the focus of senior managers' attention and concern well after the rest of the organization experiences what's happening and reacts in a variety of self-defensive ways.

Defensive actions, when taken in haste or insecurity, can add to workplace instability, enlarging the challenge for senior managers to unscramble what happened and precisely how it happened.

Actions needed to stop the damaging behaviors are thus delayed because senior management is, more often than not, the last to know.

The Five Percent Impact

As noted above, a gap exists in all companies between expectation and execution.

The main focus of this book is about conflict in the workplace, but conflict is only the result of one element in the Negative Behavior Equation. As I noted above, in these pages I offer the hypothesis that the negative behaviors that drive conflict are a magnet that attracts other negative behaviors.

Unresolved conflict, unethical behavior, and unsafe acts are the primary ingredients in the Negative Behavior Equation.

30

More importantly, my hypothesis places the source of undesired or unethical behaviors inside the gap between expectation and execution in fact, almost at the source.

I will discuss this important gap in more detail later in this book. What needs to be repeated here is that not all conflict is bad. Conflicts are an inherent part of human interaction. Many times, it is the catalyst for creative solutions that successfully advance and benefit a company or organization.

Yet, one can't forget that behavior is one of the most visible examples of interaction, and behaviors drives conflict. Within any organization, 1001 conflicts will flare up and more than 95% of them will be resolved right there. Then people will move on.

It's the remaining 4.5 to 5.0 percent about which dozens of books have been written, including this one. What makes this book different? For one, it is not intended to be prescriptive. A quick look at the table of contents will demonstrate that point.

My intention here is to offer a practical workplace resource with insights of real value, which the reader can use to master conflict resolution.

For those of you old enough to appreciate the analogy, there is a big difference between a series of topographical maps and a set of Rand-McNally Roadmaps.

Similarly, there is a large difference between a world map pinned to someone's wall, and a map of a particular state in the U.S. Likewise, a solution to a conflict does not lie in the details etched into a blueprint; but in the clues the blueprint provides.

The analogy of a roadmap is a useful way of looking at conflict for one basic reason. Conflicts that fall within the five percent that can significantly disrupt the workplace never arrive unannounced.

Such troublesome conflicts provide ample warning signs along the way to the crisis point, yet most managers and supervisors miss these warnings because they haven't been trained to read the work environments they are responsible for in this manner.

Chapter 3

The Emotions Trap

People often ignore factors or circumstances that surround disagreements, and when they do, disagreements escalate into conflict. Delay resolution too long and the conflict becomes intractable. Once this happens, a successful outcome is harder to reach.

Notice I used the word "disagreements." The words conflict, disagreement, dispute, are used interchangeably, but they don't have the same meaning. As you read this book I will offer my take on why people, especially in a business environment, need to appreciate the true meaning of each word. The differentiation is important in the broader context of conflict resolution.

To get back to my starting point, why do people avoid disagreements? In most cases, it's because of apprehension and uncertainty, like approaching a house of cards and wondering if the card in your hand will be the one that causes it all to collapse.

Life has conditioned us emotionally to see disagreement with a negative perspective, as something to be avoided or prevented. More than 50 years of research provides compelling evidence that emotions strongly shape most decision making, are a key driver of behavior, and are often the impetus behind conflicts not only in the workplace but even between companies.

Emotions are not uniformly negative, however, as both science and history teach us. Strong emotions can drive people to achieve extraordinary things; even anger can generate positive outcomes.

But the converse is equally true, in that emotions such as anger, shame and resentment can create a negative and damaging workplace environment and often are the drivers behind workplace conflicts.

Psychologist John D. Mayer argues that emotions carry a physical aspect when they bridge thought, feeling, and action. Emotion can impact a person's physiology both positively and negatively, depending on the type and level of stress being felt at the moment.

Anyone confronted by a demanding task coupled with a critical timeline has certainly experienced this simple truth. Managers and supervisors often fail to recognize that decisions people make in the workplace are judged, by those making the decision or taking the action, on the basis of the risk to themselves. Perceived personal risk strongly influences decisions as well as actions.

A person who feels anxious about the impact of an outcome on him-or-herself may choose a more conservative approach, may involve others, may take longer to execute the task, and potentially may sacrifice the best outcome for one that is safe.

A Negative Work Environment Will Drive Additional Negative Behaviors.

Choosing the safe path can lead an employee at any level to doing only the minimum, so as to stay "under the radar." Such cautious behavior can, in turn, lead to other more damaging behaviors such as missing schedules, making excuses, or asking others to do the work assigned.

Awareness by managers and supervisors of those situations where emotions can have an adverse effect on the work is critical to their ability to maintain group cohesiveness and the essential productivity to achieve necessary outcomes.

Management must be able to react in a constructive way to reduce the potential for conflict without increasing anxiety and uncertainty.

It is the play-it-safe mentality that frequently drives avoidance of disagreements. The emotions that underlie that reluctance may then drive disagreements to become disputes, and, ultimately, intractable conflict.

Serious, unmitigated or intractable conflicts leave emotional scars. In an article some years ago, I wrote about the emotions that are connected to most conflicts and how those emotions can interfere with both a timely solution, and one that satisfies the interests and needs of the individuals most directly involved.

The reason it becomes so difficult to effectively manage conflicts once they escalate is surprisingly simple.
You cannot overcome another person's emotional investment without taking the time to separate the person (i.e. his/her fear, shame, anger and other feelings) from the issue. Once

someone invests emotion in a point of view or position, changing that person's attitude becomes a difficult, unpredictable challenge.

Evidence is all around us

A quick look at what we see playing out in our communities and in the country provides broad and ample evidence of how hard that process can be. We also can narrow our focus to the business world and see the outcome of conflicts that haven't been successfully resolved. The reasons almost always reflect a failure to overcome the parties' emotional investment in a disputed issue.

A typical type of unresolved conflict in companies and industries is labor strikes. Another is mergers. Both are fraught with conflict because careers and livelihoods are on the line. While these kinds of conflict make the news, they are not even the tip of the iceberg.

Look around your own company or department and, if you pay attention, you'll notice things not running as smoothly as you initially believed they are. The signs of potential conflict are there, but most people aren't trained to recognize them for what they are.

Are employees in the department competitive in an obvious way?
Just about everyone is taught that competition is a good thing, but there is fundamental truth in the old adage that too much of a good thing is harmful.

When employees in a group or department become too competitive, the energy can become a symptom of emotional rivalry. In a highly charged environment where employees become excessively competitive, teamwork collapses. This in turn introduces another group of behaviors that are mostly negative.

Unresolved Conflict Erodes Group Cohesion

Are you uncertain of your management team, and as a consequence, are you trying to "fly under the radar"? This defense mechanism is not uncommon when employees find themselves working for managers that are never around, or who are known to excessively criticize an employee's work.

In an environment where conflict percolates beneath the surface, and goes unresolved, a series of behaviors can build up and continue almost unnoticed. Tension and uncertainty force people in that department to adjust here, bend there, and make a hasty assortment of compromises to get things done.

When you go home from such an uneasy environment at the end of the day, you take with you a lingering sense of dissatisfaction with yourself, your job and some of the people you work with. Your day did not go as well as you wanted. That feeling of discontent builds up and eventually impacts your performance, your dedication, and your commitment.

Imagine those same negative emotions spread throughout a department. How can they not result in conflicts?

Small, unresolved conflicts can eventually hatch larger, more widespread conflict that erodes group cohesion, damages professional relationships, and can even damage the organization. People's emotions quite naturally sustain conflict and the negative feelings it causes, but once you recognize that, you can begin the process of unwinding the issues that created the conflict in the first place.

3 Points of a Triangle

In my work I talk about this unwinding process in terms of a triangle. Some of you who read my newsletter know that I've written about this issue from time to time. I try not to repeat myself, and to instead look at different ways of making these essential points, but for anyone new to the concept, the three points of the triangle are: Separation, Explanation, and Criteria.

1. SEPARATION: Successful conflict resolution almost always begins by bringing each side's assumptions out into the open. The emotional investment I talk about here is, more often than not, supported by assumptions; mostly about the other parties in the dispute. Bringing those assumptions to light is the first step in separating fact from fiction and separating the individuals from their emotions.

2. EXPLANATION: The manager, or the person facilitating the process can then present a set of questions that allows the people involved to explain their issues in detail. The explanation process introduces clarity, and clarity generates understanding.

This is not a step where one party agrees or accepts what the other party wants. It is the point where each side understands the other. The foundation for conversation is thus built.

3. CRITERIA: The triangle's third corner is what I call the criteria step. Once a foundation for dialogue is built, potential solutions require clearly identified criteria that will allow solutions to advance in a manner the people can see and evaluate objectively.

This is the crux of the process. The triangle has to be more than a drawing on a page or white board. The process requires that the parties to the conflict take action in a controlled manner that leads to a successful resolution.

A controlled action has key components, including, but not necessarily limited to:

> A written plan is jointly developed, with everyone involved in the conflict agreeing to the plan. (consensus over compromise)
> The basis for measuring results is built into the plan
> Key decision makers are identified early and their roles are equally clear
> Ownership of outcomes is a commitment established at the beginning

Work environments damaged by conflict can be healed and the integrity of the organization restored.

Those directly involved in the conflict, and those brought in to assist, need to recognize that this process is not without consequences. In my work with clients I keep two concepts in mind: equity and prudence.

I emphasize these two concepts because, in today's environment, people accept the idea of collateral damage far too easily. I have immense distaste for solutions that clear the field without any thought for the damage to innocent by-standers.

An underappreciated aspect to the origins of many conflicts is one of my reasons for writing this book. Each chapter is based in part on the training modules I developed as part of my work assisting companies dealing with a range of conflicts.

I have expanded those training-focused ideas to reflect an analysis that attempts to show a complete fabric with important concepts identified. My objective is that those reading this book can follow the major threads and make sense of the whole.

I find it interesting that a number of people in my profession take the position that conflict resolution is akin to walking through an emotional minefield. That seems an interesting way to justify taking a stronger hand – an excuse to lead rather than guide. The implication in that point of view is that emotions didn't matter until the conflict developed, which ignores the central point that emotions are at play before a conflict manifests.

This, I think, is a result of a proliferation of fads and self-help ideas that are not supported by data to any meaningful degree. As I noted at the start of this chapter, a great deal of solid research exists in the social sciences that is of benefit to those whose job it is to assist others in resolving conflict.

It also must be noted that the proliferation of fads of all kinds have greatly complicated the field.

Recognizing that much of what we read today has precious little science behind it, a serious practitioner in this field won't be successful unless he or she takes the time to study what is available, assess it, and extract from the detritus those points that have value. The challenge is to find useable ideas within psychology and sociology that do have solid data behind them.

Positive Emotions Evoke Positive Actions

I recently came across an article backed by solid research on the use of what is called "positive" psychology. The research suggests that techniques which place people in a positive frame of mind serve to create positive emotions when addressing conflict, whether in the workplace or elsewhere.

The idea I extracted from the article is that actively managing one's emotions helps create a constructive environment for resolving conflict. I was initially skeptical, but was willing to explore this article further, and once I did, the light bulb blinked on.

The Point of Convergence: A Path to Understanding Conflict Resolution

All of us look at situations, concepts, developments and other things, either concrete or intangible, and when we see something that is obvious to us, we say to ourselves...come on guys, use a little common sense! The article on positive psychology began to make sense to me because it talked in an organized way about the thing we call common sense.

One cannot be successful in resolving a conflict if one does not have self-awareness as a starting point. Identifying key roles of those involved in a conflict begins with understanding your own role.

Once you have placed yourself in the proper perspective, you can look at and speak about such concepts as the integrity of the process, the key values, and the discipline of positive remarks over negative remarks, and the insistence on active listening and respect.

Place each of these ideas inside a circle where all the circles connect, and lo-and- behold, you have a common sense approach to conflict resolution that actually does advance the resolution of conflicts which arise in your arena, can prevent many conflicts from occurring, or at the very least can mitigate them at an early stage.

Emotions in a work environment can be both a minefield and a trap, but only if one walks into an emotional situation carelessly. Being aware of one's workplace environment is a basic obligation, and that means awareness of the emotions at play in that work space as well.

The Point of Convergence: A Path to Understanding Conflict Resolution

Being aware of unspoken forces strengthens your place in the group, strengthens your performance, and most telling of all, has an outsized effect on your ability to make good decisions.

Chapter 4

Recognizing the Disagreement

Disagreements are everywhere. You find them at home, at work, at church, and occasionally, among strangers. The majority of disagreements are never fully resolved. People will go to great lengths to avoid dealing with a disagreement.

At home couples develop a range of coping mechanisms until the disagreement eventually escalates, and some action needs to be taken. At work, employees go to great lengths to "not get involved". To varying degrees companies spend significant resources each year in an effort to motivate employees to deal with disagreements. This is done under various types of programs, under different names, and few of these efforts produce any lasting results.

Surveys taken between 2005 and 2019 show no major changes in employees' attitude towards disagreements in the workplace. They were reluctant to get involved more than a decade ago, and they are still as reluctant today as they were then. What is it that makes an employee afraid to invest himself in helping resolve a disagreement?

Workers are experts at avoidance. In the workplace, disagreements aren't resolved because people are afraid of putting themselves at risk if they try.
It is not groundbreaking news that most of us are never taught any sort of consistent strategy for addressing negative or confrontational situations either at home or at work.

44

The Point of Convergence: A Path to Understanding Conflict Resolution

Some parents are good at rearing their children to deal in constructive ways with the underlying conflicts in the home, most of which begin with a disagreement that arises among family members and/or friends. Most parents, however, either do poorly or provide inconsistent guidance. As a consequence, our young adults enter the workforce without the faintest clue how to resolve workplace conflict, and very few tools exist in the workplace that gives employees the confidence to try.

For example, if you ask the average twenty-something employee to explain what a disagreement is, that person will, more often than not, provide a rambling explanation that wanders all over the map. No one bothered to explain early on that a disagreement is nothing more than "an absence of consensus". It's a simple uncomplicated definition, but as everyone quickly learns, the simple things in life are hardest to master.

This reflects an important truth almost always ignored or misunderstood by people facing a set of circumstances where they don't agree over what action(s) to take. As a general rule, employees want to believe the best of themselves, but when it comes to this most basic concept, they will do their best to evade it. To use a military expression, they will "duck and cover" instead of dealing with the disagreement. They do so out of fear.

What most employees react to, and why the parties are afraid to get involved, is they don't want to be seen as being wrong, or uncooperative, or not a team player.

What they also don't know is that, at the time of the disagreement, no one is right and no one is wrong. Individuals simply see certain issues differently, and the issues important to one are not as important to another member of the team.

The fear of most individuals involved in a disagreement is that they may be perceived as doing the wrong thing, thereby making things worse, so they stand on the ground they know. It escapes them that both sides are right at the point the disagreement arises. One person's way of processing information and dealing with issues is different from someone else's method.

The differing points of view create, at first, confusion, and it is in working through this initial confusion where things can go wrong. In the many conflicts that flare up briefly in the workplace, the vast majority go through an initial confusion stage and are resolved – some smoothly, others like a train that jerks and starts, jerks again, then finally moves smoothly forward.

The disagreement becomes evident when movement from initial confusion does not progress to the next step toward resolution. Instead, what comes out of that initial confusion is two parties that see only one solution – their own.

The Hidden Drivers

In general, people understand diverse perceptions are the seeds of brilliance in a think tank or a brainstorming situation. Unhappily, however, they also are the drivers behind most conflicts, in the workplace and elsewhere. A quick trip to the internet will easily identify a half dozen or more drivers that show up in the types of conflicts we see in our workplaces. In this chapter I touch on one of several psychological truths about what people perceive and how they process their perceptions.

One such driver is, "why does this keep happening?" The person or persons asking this are subconsciously stating "it's not my fault. The boss needs to look somewhere else because "I'm doing my job just fine, and I get along fine with everyone." How often have we heard – or thought – this sort of deflection when we experience conflict around us?

This defense mechanism is almost always a subjective reflex, because most of us are not aware that a conflict is brewing until it erupts almost in front of our noses. I make note of this lack of awareness periodically in my blog posts and in my monthly newsletter. On reflection, I believe employees are often more aware than they will admit, but are surprised at the suddenness of the eruption.

Conflict rarely arrives unannounced. The weatherman on your TV gives his viewers regular updates of a significant change in the weather, advising viewers to be prepared. And people prepare themselves.

Like those weather forecasts, conflicts that invade a work environment also come with warning signs, which can be easily recognized by those who know what to look for.
My experience tells me most employees are more attuned to their work environments than they realize. They may spend

most of their time focused on their tasks, but they are not oblivious to those things that make for a difficult environment. They see the warning signs, they interpret them, yet they don't prepare.

Why don't they prepare? I believe it's because they don't see themselves as the authors of any potential solutions to problems that may lie festering in the weeds. This perceived absence of freedom to act creates a sense of frustration, so they armor themselves with the It's-not-my-fault defense, making it somebody else's problem.

As noted earlier fear is always a motivating factor. Seeing conflict developing, and reacting to a developing situation, is not the same as reacting to a conflict once it begins to impact the work environment. Reacting to a developing situation is far riskier than confronting one that is already in plain view.

Think about it. Heading off a conflict before it becomes a problem is very similar to building a fire break to bring wildfire under control. Building a firebreak, however, requires planning and a degree of skill, and like a firebreak, conflict prevention is not something you can do by yourself.

You have to involve other people, but involving others in what you see as a developing conflict can be interpreted by those around you as whistleblowing.

It does not matter what you see on television about the importance of whistleblowers, and it does not matter what your particular company's senior leaders say about the importance of hearing the truth from employees – that they

48

will be protected if they come forward. The cold hard truth is that confronting a nascent conflict requires informing others and gaining their participation, and it will be perceived as whistleblowing, and that puts the employee's future at risk.

When it comes to conflict, few people want to put themselves on the firing line (pun intended). The fact that most employees notice the conflict happening around them is also not in question. That most go to great lengths not to get personally involved is a well-established fact. It takes an employee with unusual courage to tackle a conflict in the workplace that everyone else is ignoring.

When I sit down with a client, I use stories and relatable situations to help them feel more at ease with this subject. I often use potholes in the street as a metaphor for the disagreement. A pothole is a very good metaphor to understand the way people process beliefs.

All of us see potholes in our streets every day. In some parts of the city I live in, Houston, they are more prevalent than in others. This is a common characteristic of most cities, and you can draw your own conclusion as to why that is.

The important fact is that you rarely get from point A to point B in a large city without encountering a pothole. What do you do? What do I do? We drive around the pothole, doing our best to avoid it.

We do this because we see it as someone else's responsibility. Yes, there are those concerned citizens who will call the public works department and report the damaged road, and when nothing happens immediately they will call back. They are the exception, because most people just complain to themselves, their fellow passenger, or their co-worker about the lousy road conditions.

A pothole in the company parking lot is a different matter. Employees driving into a parking lot with potholes will inform their supervisor, or they'll make calls to the plant maintenance people or to whoever is in charge of interfacing with the property owner. The response in this circumstance is different because the employee is not afraid to speak out.

A majority of people approach potholes in the street the same way they approach disagreements in the workplace; they see it as someone else's problem. The reason they walk around a problem at work, jump over it, take a detour, and generally do whatever they can to pass it off to someone else comes down to one thing – who takes the first step.

Filling a pothole or solving a disagreement ultimately means someone makes the final decision, but getting there relies on one key word – consensus.

Consensus is not easy, which is why most in the workplace default to what is most comfortable.
For example, managers and supervisors in one department will listen to and work with managers and supervisors in another department to accommodate one another's needs.

Both departments have goals and objectives that are compatible and some that are not compatible. Areas of non-compatibility require that the department managers and supervisors work through potential areas of conflict and reach a compromise. By striking a compromise, the managers are able to reach an agreement that allows the work of both departments to proceed.

Sounds reasonable doesn't it, but does it really work?

Consensus v. Compromise

Reaching a consensus and reaching a compromise are not the same thing. The reason so many disagreements remain unresolved and eventually escalate to conflicts, is that achieving a consensus means everyone has to agree to a path forward; a compromise does not solve the disagreement. Consensus building is time consuming, and frustrating, and busy managers are often too impatient to allow this process to unfold the way it needs to.

Getting two or more people to agree on a single course of action is a challenge in any work environment. Yes, some companies actively encourage consensus building because they know it makes their work environments more stable, and their employees more focused on their tasks.
Encouraging consensus does not necessarily produce successful outcomes, but it does make agreement easier.

In many companies, the goal is getting the job done, and the default position is to compromise to the extent needed to advance the work. These companies didn't get the memo that the most lasting solution to any conflict is to deal with it at the point where and when the argument is first identified. That first identification is the point where two or more people determine they are not in agreement on a path forward.

In Chapter Two I describe the anatomy of a conflict and the importance of understanding how unresolved differences will escalate; sometimes slowly but sometimes with stunning rapidity. I don't intend to re-argue what I wrote earlier.

The power of disagreements to sow the seeds of discord, however, is such that this book can't be as effective as I want it to be unless you, the reader, understand what needs to happen and how it needs to happen.

The Critical Break Point

From my perspective, not enough people in leadership roles give enough importance to that point where a lack of consensus occurs. Potential conflicts resolved at this critical point have a powerful and positive effect on work environments.

More often than not, unfortunately, I see what I call "too soon and too late." What do I mean by this?
Earlier, I noted that when two or more people find they do not agree on a path forward, no one is right and no one is wrong; they simply see things differently.

The point where this lack of consensus is identified is not the point where a manager or supervisor should demand compromise. It is too soon.

At this point, the parties have not had a chance to explore at what part or parts of the problem the differences of opinion emerge. Yet, it is at this point that managers and supervisors begin to assert pressure to find a solution and move forward, and if someone on the team does not "give in" and go along with others, the manager is all too ready to pick a solution that the majority of the team supports.

Once the decision is made, the team will be comprised of winners and losers. That dynamic cannot be undone; it is now too late in the process to undo that damage.

Consensus building is a learned skill, and equally important it is a skill where timing matters. In the dynamic surrounding a disagreement the opportunity exists to work towards consensus, but time waits for no man, and if that opportunity is not grasped, it is lost.

By way of an exercise, look at a conflict you were involved with at work. Consider writing out two lists. On one list you write down all the misperceptions about that conflict.

On the other list write down perceptions about the conflict that appear to be true. When compared, the misperceptions will outnumber the true perceptions by a significant margin.

The reality is that almost all perceptions will address the origin of the conflict, what drives the conflict, how to do something about it, and how to most effectively prevent similar conflict. Very little, on either list, will help leaders or employees understand the emotional dynamic that surrounds the disagreement.

The Point of Convergence: A Path to Understanding Conflict Resolution

Chapter 5

Discovering the Issues

Knowledge comes, but wisdom lingers. It may not be difficult to store up in the mind a vast quantity of facts within a comparatively short time, but the ability to form judgments requires the severe discipline of hard work and the tempering heat of experience and maturity. (Calvin Coolidge)

A workplace is defined by its "environment". Most of us encountering this word are conditioned by popular culture to apply it primarily to the natural world; as in "a clean or polluted environment". Businesses are not separate from the world in which their employees live, but represent part of the modern human eco-system. And like many eco-systems found in nature, businesses have multiple environments.

All business environments are unstable. This is a clear and simple truth, since all businesses are either growing, contracting, becoming stagnant, or failing. Anyone who claims to work in a stable company or who claims to enjoy their current job because everybody gets along, would be surprised to learn that the space they occupy is not static.

Instability in the workplace is unavoidable, and workers who recognize that instability fall into two camps.

Some see it as a problem to be solved, and they try to stabilize their work environments.

In due course they will fail, because they don't yet understand that the element creating the instability is energy – produced by human emotions.

First Camp

It is human emotion that drives both success and failure. Nevertheless, workers in this first camp vigorously seek conformity in as many aspects of their work environments as possible. In doing so, they often misunderstand where conformity is effective and where it isn't.

Without question, any company needs its employees at all levels to accept and commit themselves to the values the company espouses through its Code of Conduct. The code, also commonly called *the standards* of conduct, typically details both the "do's and the don'ts" company employees are required to comply with.

Conformity of behavior to those standards is not theoretical. It is a clear and objective conduct that leaders, managers, supervisors, and employees are expected to adopt.

This need for conformity rightfully extends to processes and procedures on which the quality and reliability of products and service depends in order for a company to compete successfully in the marketplace. Conformity to standard, whether in conduct or in an operational setting, reduces errors.

Second Camp

Emotions can't be forced into conformity.

Employees who fall into the second camp understand that instability exists naturally in any work environment and seek to harness that energy in positive ways. Leaders and managers in this camp also recognize that work environments need consistent maintenance to prevent natural instability from expanding beyond their control.

A majority of management's motivational efforts result from the understanding by company leaders that individual employees need one another's support, and that group cohesion requires everyone in the group to pitch in – at least to some degree.

The idea that everyone pitches in doesn't change as companies grow over time. The human dynamic may change, the degree to which everyone works together may change, but the basic idea remains.

As the writer Clay Clark notes in a recent article, the need for members of a team to "have each other's back" is especially true at the start-up stage. Clark states "...in the startup work environment, you get to have a relationship with your boss, the investors, and the key members of the team. Startups are like families - you see the good, the bad and the ugly, but in the end, you've got each other's back..."

Companies spend significant amounts of money on a wide range of tools and techniques to motivate employees to behave better, to perform better, and for entire groups to function better.

The goal of the second camp is to prevent work environments from becoming more unstable. They may not think about it precisely in those terms, but leaders know that decreasing workplace stability creates conflict.

Elements that Drive Conflict

In a nutshell, that's what this book is about – the elements inside work environments that drive conflict. An important distinction exists between the types of conflict that drives individuals and teams to achieve more, create better products, and ultimately change things for the better, and the types of conflict that drives disruptive behaviors, thus decreasing or, in a worst case, shattering workplace stability.

What are the destabilizing elements that impact thousands of departments and groups every day? Just about everyone has heard the phrase "toxic work environment" and can give easy examples, such as poor workplace habits, inconsistent application of policies, and offering false compliments.

What about the less obvious examples – the ones with the power to truly damage relationships and bring serious harm to an organization?

Workers at all levels occasionally complain about favoritism. While they may offer anecdotal examples of what they perceive as favoritism; few truly understand how destabilizing it can be if allowed to take root.

Favoritism impacts how one's work is perceived. How many of us have seen someone do good work only to have someone else's less valuable work given more visibility?

Have you ever had your own work diminished because someone felt threatened by what you did? When things happen, the hard truth is that competent people doing solid work will be denied the raises and promotions they deserve, and favoritism is often at the root of such behaviors.

The existence of obvious favoritism is a motivating factor in the formation of cliques. Employees begin to feel left out of key decisions and develop a perception that information is being withheld from them.

Real or imagined, these suspicions drive down productivity, are a significant factor in the increase of mistakes, and are also a catalyst for turnover.

Nepotism is favoritism dressed up in a different suit. Nepotism is easy to spot, and its impact on the workplace is predictable. Because it involves family, this kind of preferential treatment, along with its negative impact, can usually be understood and adjusted to, if not necessarily accepted.

A less obvious negative behavior is competition that gets out of hand. Excessive competition doesn't merely destabilize a work environment. It is one of those elements that promote workplace toxicity. This particular poison damages a work environment gradually until it becomes too obvious to ignore.

People wake up to the fact they are playing a zero sum game where it isn't the results that's being measured, but the performance as well.

No two people get to the end result in exactly the same way, and grading the performance of one versus another creates a winners and losers workplace. Most won't put up with that for very long before they start trying to stack the deck in their favor.

Like conflict, competition is crucial to the success of any organization. Most of us are taught as early as grade school that competition is a good thing. It generally is seen as healthy among co-workers and healthy for the work environment. As I note in other books and articles, however, the wrong kind of conflict is harmful, and so too is the wrong kind of competition.

When employees in a group or department become too competitive, it is a symptom of something much larger. In a highly charged environment where employees become excessively competitive, team work collapses.

Co-workers become competitors in a way that reflects the classic us-versus-them mentality, the healthy team dynamic sours and in turn, introduces another group of behaviors that are mostly negative. When such behaviors are not reined in by the company's leadership, these new negative behaviors will impact how leaders are perceived by the rank and file.

As employees become uncertain about their management team, they will start to look at where they are at risk. They will protect themselves in various ways by trying to "fly under the radar", or going to the other extreme by seeing the outcome as the prize.

They feel compelled to win at all costs; even through cheating, or damaging the efforts of those they view as the competition.

Once conflict is added to a business environment, all problems become much more impactful. As noted previously, conflict exists naturally in organizations. Much of it is either positive, neutral, or slightly negative. But watch out! When it moves from slightly negative to markedly negative, the impact can be dramatic.

I am no longer surprised by how few people understand the speed at which a conflict can escalate. Also, I think too many people see examples of conflict that have been around for a long time, or look at conflicts from an institutional perspective, such as labor strikes or other similar disputes, and draw the wrong kinds of lessons from that anecdotal evidence.

Most of us have experienced conflict that lingers for long periods of time, simmering just below the surface, and only flaring up occasionally, while never being completely resolved. This universal experience creates an understanding that deceives people and, in the workplace, may lead them to draw wrong conclusions about how they should respond to conflicts that erupt.

A group might recognize conflict that is disrupting the work environment, yet do nothing to mitigate the situation. This inertia exposes an "it's-not-my-job" syndrome.

The Typical early response is to try and work around the conflict, or engage in other avoidance techniques. Often, nothing changes the situation right away.

In fact, all this avoidance allows the conflict to escalate until urgent action is needed or the conflict will become intractable. At this point, reaching a successful outcome is difficult, and even when one finally does come about, these kinds of conflicts leave emotional scars.

Skewed Perceptions

Perception is a powerful thing. It is through our perceptions that we manage our way through life's daily demands. "Perceiving," in its classic definition is "the state of being or process of becoming aware of something through the senses". Perception, then, is defined as "a way of regarding, understanding, or interpreting something by intuition and insight".

Simple? Yes, but how people understand the concept of perception is at odds with how they apply it. A flaw of perception, as I term it, is the widely held notion that people's behaviors are driven by a rational understanding of the world around them. They perceive their actions and decisions to be based on rational behaviors.

When informed that their behaviors are a product of their emotions, many become upset and defensive. In their minds, reason and rationality guide their actions and decisions. Certainly, they are not emotion-driven.

Successful leaders become successful because they master the ability to persuade, influence, and motivate the employees working in their organizations.

Motivation doesn't happen through the language of logic and reason, however, those come later. Successful leaders appeal to what makes employees feel valued.

By ignoring, dismissing, or making light of those things that feed emotional well-being we create opportunities for negative behaviors. As I've said in previous texts, trust is a fragile thing, and when a leader is perceived as ignoring or making light of things that concern the employees, they will, as individuals and as a group, initiate a whole series of defensive behaviors in response.

Distorted Communication

In her book *What Keeps Leaders Up at Night*, Dr. Nicole Lipkin writes about what happens when leaders lose the ability to communicate with their employees. She describes it as the Cassandra Conundrum, which comes to us through Greek Mythology.

Simply stated, the legend tells us about a woman who was given the power of prophesy, but because she was not properly grateful, the gift came with a curse -- whatever she prophesied, no one would hear. Dr. Lipkin noted that, once a leader fails his or her employees when it matters, whatever the leader says in the future will fall on deaf ears.

Employees will then respond defensively to perceptions that take hold and will not see until it's too late that some of the conflicts created in their work environments are driven by their own behaviors.

Employees who do see their part in the conflicts tend to become even more defensive and accusatory, as they begin to build their "fortifications," metaphorically speaking.

It is at this point that leaders need to start the communication process again, this time with great care. Otherwise, any communication that is initiated will accomplish little or nothing.

In work environments where conflict goes unresolved, communication isn't about getting things done.

This is where individuals begin talking over each other, going around each other, and working at cross purposes. Communication becomes the vehicle by which the combatants in a conflict build and bolster their defenses.

They defend their conflicting positions before giving any consideration on how it affects the work. Any criticism or complaint, no matter how small, becomes an imperative that must first be defended against and then challenged.

In this environment-gone-awry, it is critical that positive and encouraging statements be maximized and that body language fully complement spoken language. Any perceived disconnect between the words being used, and the speaker's gestures or facial expressions, will damage any effort to deconstruct the employees' defenses, and the efforts to mediate the conflict resolution will quickly lose credibility.

Social scientists have developed a significant body of empirical data that suggests non-verbal communication often sends messages more clearly than words.

When I am asked by clients to assist in resolving workplace conflict, this is an area I focus on almost immediately. I emphasize the importance of choosing carefully how words are used, by whom and where, then review any non-verbal elements that might undermine their efforts.

Negative, rash or uncertain body language can entirely undermine someone's best efforts to resolve a dispute. One suggestion I frequently make to managers and supervisors is to always hold conflict discussions with everyone sitting in a straight-backed chair.

Nothing robs a manager's credibility quicker than confronting agitated and uncertain employees who are seated in rigid "visitor chairs", while the manager can swivel, roll away or lean back. Nothing creates a more powerful message of "I am not as involved in this as you" or even worse "I am really being patient here so let's hurry it up".

Confronting resistance directly generally doesn't work, anyway, because trust dissolves when conflict goes unresolved. Experience has shown me frequently that an indirect approach can be more effective in restarting the conversation.

The Point of Convergence: A Path to Understanding Conflict Resolution

In the next chapter and later I will introduce the theory that metaphors and analogies offer an effective way of alleviating the distrust and suspicions that surround most entrenched conflict.

Chapter 6

Constructing the Conversation

The real art of conversation is not only to say the right thing at the right place but to leave unsaid the wrong thing at the tempting moment. (Dorothy Nevill)

Let's begin with the idea that people, in general, do not understand how to have meaningful conversations. It doesn't matter whether you're in a business setting or private life somewhere. Most of us get it wrong at one time or another, and some more than most.

Conversations in a business environment generally have better outcomes than in other areas because most conversations in business revolve around getting work done. Yet, those involved in workplace conversations often have reasons for guarding what they say and careful about who they speak with about certain topics. Unfortunately, self-imposed restrictions often diminish the effectiveness of these discussions. Cautious behaviors multiply when people find themselves in an environment rife with conflict.

It's certainly easy to understand that conflict makes people uncomfortable. Disputes are hard for many of us to navigate, so we avoid dealing with them. In disputes within companies, the level of discomfort may make face-to-face discussion an unrealistic goal. Consequently, many third-party neutrals engaged in resolving conflicts find themselves using caucus-only conversations.

Out of an excess of concern, companies tend to support this shuttle style mediation. It is too soon to say whether this method is becoming standard practice, but it does suggest potential problems for practitioners down the road. The problem with this approach is that conversations designed to disarm conflict don't happen when the parties are not in the same room.

The first goal of a third-party neutral, or mediator, is to keep the parties in dispute in the same space – when it's safe to do so. The second goal is to control the environment. Later in this chapter, I will touch on the importance of the umpire versus-referee challenge.

The environment in which people convene has a direct impact on how well conversations play out. When conflict disrupts the workplace, and the people involved stop speaking with one another in any meaningful way, key personnel must recognize their broken processes are part of the problem. At this point, fixing what's broken requires a process outside the normal.

Once a selected third-party neutral has prepared the conflict resolution environment, it is time to understand what is driving the conflict. Even at this early stage, specific steps must occur in the right order. Any conversation has to have both a foundation and a context. In my work, I spent a lot of time focusing on those two components.

Simply stated, in a conflict situation, constructing the conversation is a necessary first step.

There are specific steps to building this type of conversation and skipping any of the steps will make solving the conflict more difficult. Also, success requires that those involved use language with care and, many times, in an artful manner. By "artful," I mean that a direct head-on approach will not work because the levels of distrust will not allow it.

Any conversation to advance the resolution of conflict or dispute must begin with the idea of disarming distrust. This means the mediator, the person who guides or facilitates the resolution process, needs to have a plan that outlines how and when the parties address particular issues.

Alleviating Doubt and Suspicion

The dilemma most apparent when dealing with a conflict situation is the absence of trust. That central reality can't be confronted directly. Individuals involved in the conflict will be too suspicious, too wary, especially during the opening minutes of discussion. Asking them to set aside their defense mechanisms too quickly will not work.

The challenge here is to persuade the parties to behave and speak differently about the topic than the discordant feelings percolating in their hearts and minds might demand – and this won't happen in the first hour. The person or team mediating a dispute will need to build the conversation around ideas and examples the parties understand. This is why analogies and metaphors are powerful tools for those venturing into the conflict arena.

The proof behind the process is that point when the parties in conflict understand what you want them to hear – when they realize what you are communicating and its essential significance. Understanding precedes action. Understanding leads to acceptance of what is said, and this happens because of the ideas and examples used to reach that common perception.

Ideas and examples are tools that carry powerful psychological impact, and their use early in the process is essential in starting the conversation; because the first thing the parties need to do is agree on what caused the dispute. Anyone dealing with conflict understands that the parties involved, regardless of what they believe, or how long the conflict has existed; rarely agree on what caused the dispute.

Ready, Set...

A useful starting point for the conversation is when the mediator/facilitator communicates the difference between an umpire and a referee. Differences between the two are subtle but essential.

An umpire sets down the rules and makes sure they're followed, and a referee arbitrates conflicting viewpoints. In the beginning, the mediator is an umpire, and if he or she executes this correctly, then the "why" question is deferred without argument. Anything related to the "why" question is placed on the shelf and out of the way.

Once a third party arrives to assist in the resolution process, no one wants to hear explanations about what went wrong. A

70

debate at this point over why this happened or that other thing happened would simply perpetuate the controversy that led to the situation in which they now find themselves.

So the third-party neutral in this equation takes control and deflects any attempt to argue the why question until the appropriate time.

At this point, the referee steps in, and by (hopefully) adroit questioning, sets the tone for the type of open-ended questions used to form a jointly erected framework the parties can build on. I call this the Defining Stage, and it is an indispensable precursor to what follows.

Dr. Ichak Adizes of the Adizes Institute makes a similar point in one of his recent articles where he wrote "they must first agree on what they are talking about before they can discuss it before moving to a point where they either agree or disagree. Once we define what we mean by the words we use, once everyone involved knows what they are talking about, it is much easier to resolve conflict."

Dr. Adizes is right about this. Very few conflicts will advance to any degree unless the parties understand and agree to the meaning of keywords and phrases, and how they apply to issues at hand.

Experience teaches me that this essential first step can't be avoided or truncated.
When the process is followed, and none of the steps are missed or skipped, the second part of the process – the

dialogue – is now possible because the parties are no longer arguing over the meaning of something.

During the Defining Stage, you may notice people beginning to loosen up, lay down their metaphoric swords, and occasionally nod in agreement with a simple question of time or place. You may even see a smile or two. To illustrate this idea, let's look at a ball. Am I talking about a soccer ball, a basketball, a football? If I talk about the idea of a ball, it will not make sense until I give it context.

To borrow from an article I read recently..."If I say a game of catch goes nowhere unless you have a partner who catches the ball and throws it back to you, what does that mean to you?"

In that one sentence you now have a great deal more information. You now know it's not a soccer ball, and you can assume that it is not a basketball, as neither of those fits into a game of catch. Yet, not enough context exists to remove any argument over meaning. In football and baseball, catching the ball is central to both games.

The above quote that speaks to two people catching a ball is deliberately incomplete. However, if you modify the quote to say the people playing catch are wearing a ball glove, just about everyone, from child to adult, understands that two people are throwing a baseball back and forth.

Analogies, Similes, and Metaphors

72

The Point of Convergence: A Path to Understanding Conflict Resolution

The conflict resolution process almost always begins with creating a shared understanding of the starting point, and analogies are an effective way of reaching that shared understanding.

A substantial body of science backs the power of analogies and their ability to connect the similarities between objects and ideas in ways that resonate with people. Here's one from Albert Einstein – "Life is like a bicycle. To keep your balance, you must keep moving."

To quickly clear up what you might be wondering, Einstein's analogy is in the form of a simile. If he'd said, "Life *is* a bicycle..." it would have been a metaphor. The word "like" is the only difference between the two literary terms, simile, and metaphor. Both, however, are analogies.

An Analogy differs only in the sense that it may go further in describing the similarities and working them into a lengthier targeted message. What makes analogies so useful is that logic and reasoning are the foundation for the comparison of two ideas – one to the other.

Science shows us that analogous reasoning is one of the principal ways humans process their understanding. We call an analogy an argument of comparison by which the process of reasoning is carried out.

The paradox is that, while people often subconsciously use analogies to solve problems, far too few make a conscious effort to employ this tool when, where, and effectively enough to do the most good.

Also, an analogy is a powerful tool in the conflict resolution toolkit. A common perception exists that metaphors are merely a literary device used by writers of poetic prose. Indeed, writers rely on analogies, as well as their poetic cousin, the metaphor, to give life to what they write.

It does not matter if the writer is creating a fictional story with numerous potentials, plots, and settings, or writing a nonfiction book about 1001 possible subjects.

Both concepts are essential for writers to understand if they want their book or paper to capture and hold a reader's attention.

Here is a more profound truth: metaphors are the oxygen that breathes life into a story. All one needs to do is read any book by Stephen King to see how that truth applies to fiction and read Laura Hillebrand's book *Unbroken*. Metaphors are essential to storytelling.

What may surprise some is that this literary device can be an effective way of bridging differences between people who distrust each other. That the use of analogies, similes, and metaphors can help us construct a conversation that is supported by solid science.

When used correctly, a metaphor can quickly and with great style create a compelling connection between two seemingly unrelated things. I will take the risk of using a timeworn example here because it is a simple metaphor with a strong cognitive connector.

The movie Forrest Gump landed in the American consciousness about 25 years ago. Many pieces of dialogue from that movie are now parts of everyday conversation, but none has been repeated more often than the line Tom Hanks spoke while sitting on a park bench. He said, almost in passing, "Mama always said life was like a box of chocolates. You never know what you're gonna get."

The two sentences complete the metaphor, and it works because it is elegantly simple. Of course, the Robert Zemeckis film also provided the atmosphere, which a good speaker or storyteller would call "setup." Without atmosphere or setup, an otherwise good analogy can fall flat.

I've seen the Gump analogy used clumsily when a speaker converts the phrase, "life was like a box of chocolates" to present tense, then attempts to illustrate a point. The speaker usually fails to construct a meaningful conversation around the metaphor, and people see it as insincere.

Learning to use this classic literary device is well worth the time because it's an effective way of breaking down distrust. Talking about trust early is like throwing a pass in football. It can go right the first time, but there are three or four ways it can go wrong, all of them bad.

Analogy and Conflict

The goal is to link in the minds of the combatants an abstract idea with something concrete and straightforward.

The Point of Convergence: A Path to Understanding Conflict Resolution

Choosing the right metaphor and emphasizing how it's used is important because science indicates that this approach can change the way people think about a concept on an unconscious level.

To illustrate this point, I offer the following from a study conducted by Professors Paul H. Thibodeau of Oberlin College and Professor Lera Boroditsky of the University of California at San Diego. In their 2011 study, the researchers used two metaphors when describing a certain city with a historically high crime rate.

With one control group, they used an animal metaphor to describe the criminal element "preying" on innocent civilians. With a second group, the criminal element was described as a disease that "plagued" communities throughout the city.

When each group was asked to explore solutions for dealing with the criminal element, the ideas strongly reflected the metaphors used in each group. The "animal" side said the problem needed crime control strategies that involved more police, increased the penalties in the laws, and other similar policies. The "plague" control group identified treatment strategies, such as better job training programs and more inner-city jobs.

Since metaphors can change perceptions, those involved should not overlook these as a means of advancing the resolution of conflicts. A bonus to take note of is that their impact is not temporary.

The perceptions that metaphors create can endure for a significant amount of time. After a quarter of a century, moviegoers are still comparing life to a box of chocolates.

What's more, people will repeat them, in their workplace and other situations, to prevent conflict from disrupting the group, the relationship, or to diffuse one that's busy simmering.

Chapter 7

Avoid the Catapult

Trouble results when the speed of growth exceeds the rate of nurturing human resources. To use tree rings as an analogy of growth, when a tree experiences rapid growth, it can cause the rings to grow abnormally thick, and this can weaken the tree trunk, and the tree can break. (Akio Toyota)

A conflict can contain several unusual characteristics simultaneously, which is one reason it takes time to unwrap a conflict and identify the real drivers. One of those characteristics is the breakdown of communication to the point that it is no longer about getting things done. Communication ceases, and what dialogue exists becomes the vehicle by which protagonists in conflict build their defenses.

Before any consideration about how it affects the work, messages conveyed through heated glances, silence, and backroom whispers provide the means to defend their fortified positions. Any criticism or complaint, no matter how small, becomes an imperative that must first be defended against and then challenged.

It sometimes surprises the length of time this static condition endures. Those most involved in the conflict, and those at the periphery make explicit or implicit accommodations that allow conflict to fester. Workarounds and inefficiencies become the norm.

Yet, even when the conflict reaches this critical point, most do not reach the point of intractability. A real difference exists between disputes that are merely challenging and hard to resolve and conflicts that become intractable.

I offer two examples to illustrate this point. For more than 100 years, stories about the West were a common aspect of our culture, and the myths coming out of these stories captivated people around the world. As a native of Arizona, I was like many kids of that time in that I loved to read just about anything featuring adventure and drama, especially westerns.

I was about twelve when I discovered paperback novels. Suddenly my weekly allowance went toward books by western writers like Owen Wister, Luke Short, Zane Gray, Wayne Overholser, and many others. I was drawn to the battle between good and evil.

From Feuds to Battles

These exciting stories were catnip to a kid who grew up in small mountain towns with little or no access to TV or even decent radio reception. When I was fourteen, I read a book about the Tonto Basin War, also called the Pleasant Valley Wars. The bloodiest feud in America's history involved a family by the name of Tewksbury on one side and a family named Graham on the other.

The Hatfield-McCoy feud, also violent, is better known because of where the quarrel took place - at the conjunction of West Virginia, Kentucky, and the Big Sandy River. It captured the public's imagination because of its proximity to

Washington D.C. and because it was born from the passions of the Civil War. This feud would last nearly thirty years before the governors of Tennessee and West Virginia called in federal marshals and federal troops to bring things under control.

The Arizona feud lasted roughly eleven years, from 1881 to 1892, and was much more violent. Unlike the Hatfield-McCoy conflict, it caused others in the Tonto Basin to take sides, and by the time it was over, between 35 and 50 men, women, and children had died. The Graham family was completely wiped out.

Edwin Tewksbury, the second son, was the sole survivor of his family. The Tonto Basin War was the principal reason Arizona was denied statehood in 1891, and it would not see its application for statehood reviewed and accepted for more than 20 years.

What does this brief history lesson mean? It is my way of reminding readers that emotions drive conflict, even conflict in the workplace. Yes, this was a family feud, but those ranches were family businesses. Ranching was big business in Arizona, and the feud started with a business dispute. As a student of conflict, I've made a point of reading about wars and feuds, how they begin, and how they escalate. History, both bygone and current, offers a window into how conflicts play out all around us.

Feuds can escalate to the point of damaging a nation. Do I exaggerate?

Read about the War of the Roses and how it effectively reshaped England, paving the way for the Renaissance. Similarly, conflicts within a company can damage that company and reshape it in significant ways.

Reshaping an Industry

To illustrate this point further, take a look at the airline industry during the first ten to twelve years after its deregulation in 1978. The conflict between the airlines and the unions was epic. The protracted battles caused some airlines to fold, others to merge, but ultimately the union employees lost the most.

During this heated era of conflict between airlines and unions, short-sightedness seemed to rule the day. One of the most enduring examples of a union overplaying its hand during a dispute is that of the Professional Air Traffic Controllers Organization (PATCO), the air traffic controllers union.

In February of 1981, PATCO's contract with the federal government expired. The FAA and the union negotiated through most of the summer, and by August of 1981, the FAA had agreed to significant increases in pay and benefits but was unwilling to compromise on the number of hours air controllers would work (the workweek).

Because of the nature of their work, air traffic controllers could not strike.

This was a condition of their contract and also was consistent with the law. Contrary to their agreement and the law, controllers walked off the job on August 3rd, 1981.

President Reagan told them they had 48 hours to end the walk-out and return to work. PATCO's leadership sided with the members' illegal act, and President Reagan fired all of the union members, more than 11,000 workers.

Reagan then ordered the union decertified, and all future air traffic controllers would henceforth be employees of the Federal Government, would be classified as an essential service, and therefore not eligible to join any union.

These labor conflicts reshaped the industry, and there are more airline companies today than twenty years ago. They are smaller, leaner, more responsive to the demands of consumers, and thus far, it is also a safer industry.

Leaders and managers misperceive important aspects of many conflicts. It is a fundamental truth that conflict exists in the workplace and is sometimes necessary and healthy. It also is true that conflict is capable of doing more harm than good. While some conflict needs to exist, management must be vigilant and highly responsive to those factors that exacerbate potentially destabilizing conflict.

I am deeply skeptical of anyone in the conflict resolution field who argues that it is essential to manage conflict in the workplace.

The Point of Convergence: A Path to Understanding Conflict Resolution

I am sometimes frustrated by the sheer number of those offering this or that collection of recommendations for managing conflict. While they all recognize the truth that conflict exists and must be addressed, too many take the approach that it is a malady that hasn't been properly treated.

From my perspective, leaders, managers, and supervisors fail to manage the environments their employees work in, and because they do not focus on the environments, distortions and inefficiencies go unnoticed. As a consequence, conflicts take hold and grow.

Conflicts arise in the workplace every day, and 95 percent of them resolve themselves between and among those individuals closest to the disagreement. The day progresses, and the work goes on. In the five percent that is are not resolved "in real-time," two things generally happen.

Some of the unresolved conflicts float along just beneath the surface. Lingering conflicts such as these create a pressure that rises up and down. And like hot springs, every once in a while, they boil over. A supervisor/manager has to step in and smooth things over.

These types of conflict can linger for a long time, sometimes for years before they get out of hand.
They mostly go unnoticed, except for the one characteristic that defines such environments, which is turnover. If a company or organization has a department that experiences an abnormal turnover rate for several years, then the chances are that department or group has a set of issues creating an unresolved conflict.

The second thing that happens when conflict goes unresolved in real-time is that a friction point develops and becomes, metaphorically speaking, a pain point. The unresolved conflict coalesces around that point, gradually gathering strength.

The gradual change in the drivers of the conflict in this environment is rarely apparent. Most leaders and managers miss important clues because things seem to be working.
Until it doesn't.

Most of us in 6th or 7th-grade science learned about catalysts. Our teachers introduced us to the mysterious world of chemistry and kept many of us awake on warm spring afternoons by showing what happens when something new happens. That teacher introduced something into a mixture and POW! Everyone in the room is instantly awake, because what was a quiet moment of normality, suddenly isn't. Right before their eyes, something hissed, boiled, or spilled over.

What most of those kids remember is the reaction. Few might recall what was added to the ingredients to cause the event and even fewer recall that the element added was the only thing that didn't change.

That eruptive energy is what happens in most conflicts that enter an unstable condition and then resist normal diffusion and resolution efforts. When you add an outside factor, two things generally happen.

1. The outside factor is sufficient to breakdown the built-up resistance, and people begin working through the conflict.

When this occurs, repairing the work environment is now perceived as equally crucial to resolving the conflict. The two aspects seem to go hand in hand. The sad reality is this outcome occurs far less often that one would like.

2. The more common result of introducing a new factor into a simmering conflict environment is that it energizes the conflict, things speed up, and the conflict escalates. In my other writings, I've talked about the conflict that becomes intractable. Almost always, insoluble conflict results when a conflict rapidly escalates from a warm, slightly hostile environment to something a great deal hotter.

Many leaders and managers do not understand the characteristics that define various types of conflict. Some workplace conflicts have high energy. They can move from the disagreement phase to the argument, to the dispute, to a full-blown conflict, where trust blows up, and the interpersonal relationships of a department or group break down completely.

Knowing what to look for is a learned skill that does not come naturally. It is a process of learning to see what isn't obvious. For example, on large rivers, like the Mississippi River, tugboat pilots learn where dangers are and where risks might develop by studying the river's currents. The water's movement provides clear warnings, but they are usually subtle. River pilots, trained to see to these warning signs, take corrective action in time to avoid danger.

In business, leaders and managers rely on other employees to see beyond the obvious. Many of those delegated to do so are not up to the task. So the conflict grows hotter, and the environment more unstable. What surprises most people is the relative smallness of the catalyst that starts the chain reaction. It can be a word or phrase spoken carelessly or in anger. It can be a gesture, such as slamming a door.

In any environment where workers have different cultural backgrounds, differing skills with language, and approaches to problem-solving, it should come as no surprise that the triggering event is not something more dramatic. Unfortunately, it doesn't end there.

Intractable Conflict, Unstoppable Force

Now the catapult comes into play. In simple terms, it is an archaic device once used primarily in military applications to launch large stones and other missiles at an enemy's fortifications.

The thing about intractable conflicts is they don't stay contained. When a dispute reaches the catapult stage, it isn't pushed into a room somewhere and confined, although many companies try to involve Human Resources to help diffuse the situation; it often isn't enough to defuse the dispute.

At this point, regardless of what the disputing parties want, the catapult launches the issue up the chain of command.

In their eagerness to not be tainted by the failure of others, those immediately above in the chain contribute their energy to the upward momentum. The speed at which this conflict travels up the chain of command rivals the chain reaction speed that caused it to escalate in the first place.

Our analogy of the catapult is oh so very apt in this situation. Like the ancient castle walls that came tumbling down under the assault of those early catapults, once the conflict travels up the command chain, careers will fall. Sometimes it happens quickly, sometimes more slowly, but the outcome is inevitable.

Many say, as do I, that failure is the best teacher. While supervisors and managers frequently forgive minor errors, some failures carry unavoidable consequences. The failure to mitigate conflict in the environment that you work in, or perhaps supervise, reflects an unwillingness to act responsibly.

A leader unwilling to act responsibly and take the crucial steps needed to change a volatile environment in positive ways will find himself/herself looking for new career opportunities.

If one failure is common to many leaders, managers, and supervisors, it is their failure to manage effectively the environments where their employees work, and because they are not focusing on the eco-system, if you will, any distortions and inefficiencies that affect it go unnoticed.

As a consequence, conflicts take hold and simmer into full-blown eruptions.

At the most basic level, the thing that lies behind the disputes that get out of hand is the unwillingness of those involved in the conflict to act ethically and put integrity first.

When you next find yourself in a conflict-rife environment, you can be either the agent of positive change or the negative force that launches the catapult. Your integrity will be the determining factor.

A modern cousin to the catapult, the slingshot is frequently used as an analogy in business contexts. It is a useful motivational image and used as a tool to help people think about the power of teams.

Paradoxically, the catapult concept has a positive connotation in conflict resolution. This rarely used idea behind the metaphor can overcome its more common negative perspective when used correctly. Once analyzed, however, the modern catapult (slingshot) can provide a way of moving forward because the first step in working a sling is the act of pulling back.

Someone, I'm not sure who, once said, "Certain things seem to escape our notice, or they are things we've forgotten over time..." For the slingshot to work, it must be drawn back; that's the essential requirement. Nothing happens until a force is applied in pulling backward.

The pulling-back action is a slingshot's energy source, which makes this is a powerful analogy for leaders, managers, and supervisors to use in diffusing conflicts before they progress from bad to worse.

When you take the time to move the parties back to a new starting point, recognizing that the initial expenditure of time will produce significant returns, actions toward improvement that once seemed unfeasible become possible.

Chapter 8

The Criteria

"...Since everything then is cause and effect, dependent and supporting, mediate and immediate, and all is held together by a natural though imperceptible chain, which binds together things most distant and most different, I hold it equally impossible to know the parts without knowing the whole, and to know the whole without knowing the parts in detail." (Blaise Pascal)

Many who make their living by speaking at public events, or in a training environment, use the idea of a building foundation. They apply this idea as an analogy in their presentations. Those who write articles or nonfiction books also often use the concept of a foundation as an analogy for the subject of their speech.

With some exceptions, many don't spend much time talking about what goes *into* the foundation. Their goal is to connect the foundation's purpose with the idea they want to convey.

Yet what goes into a foundation *does* matter. A structure is only as good as the foundation it stands on, and those who do not take sufficient time to understand what a given foundation needs run the risk of creating a structure that won't stand over time.

Drive through a neighborhood or a business area where a house or commercial building is going up, and you'll see that the ground is prepared first, and then the foundation is poured. As you watch cement being poured and leveled, you can't know what components went into the cement mixture or what type of steel was selected to reinforce the finished concrete.

We trust that those responsible for laying the foundation prepared well in advance. They identified the criteria necessary for that foundation, including but not limited to the technical specifications for the initial mix. We trust competent people selected the correct type of steel. The success of a foundation begins well before the cement truck arrives at the construction site.

Likewise, everything necessary in a conflict-resolution process requires this same attention to detail. The steps are clear and understood well ahead of the first action. The outcome can be measured because of the attention paid to the criteria selected and the planning stages.

Let's Not Forget the Issue of Myths

Before diving into the criterion necessary for successful conflict resolution, it is appropriate to revisit myths briefly. In chapter one, I noted that many myths exist about conflicts in the workplace, and about conflict resolution in general.

I only highlighted a few of those myths as a means of setting the stage for the subject matter covered in this book. As I noted in that chapter, other myths exist that affect how people view conflict in the workplace. One of those enduring myths is the idea that all conflicts, especially those in a work environment, need to be managed.

This notion of managing all conflict endures for two reasons. One source for the myth comes from the organizational management side of things. Several theories include the idea that organizational conflict are manageable by using several steps and processes. One such theory states, in part, that:

"The management of organizational conflict involves the diagnosis of and intervention in affective and substantive conflicts at the interpersonal, intragroup, and intergroup levels and the styles (strategies) used to handle these conflicts. A diagnosis should indicate whether there is need for an intervention and the type of intervention needed.

In general, an intervention is designed to attain and maintain a moderate amount of substantive conflict in non-routine tasks at various levels, to reduce affective conflict at all levels, and to enable the organizational members to select and use the appropriate handling conflict styles so that various situations can be effectively dealt with. Organizational learning and effectiveness are enhanced through an appropriate diagnosis of and process and structural interventions in conflict". (Rahim, Garrett, & Buntzman, 1992)

As the saying goes, so good so far.

When delving deeper into these largely academic studies, however, you find the following is a fairly common conclusion…. *"1) There is no clear set of rules to suggest when conflict ought to be maintained at a certain level, when reduced, when ignored, and when enhanced, and 2) There is no clear set of guidelines to suggest how conflict can be reduced, ignored, or enhanced to increase organizational learning and effectiveness..."*

Sweep away the turgid prose that infects much of academic writings, what this says is that few conflicts, if any, are manageable within a given process. Left unsaid in many of these studies is what happens while the social scientists experiment.

Surprisingly, even in the absence of any practical model, the idea of managing conflict is widely accepted. The problem one finds is that in any given organization, a company's processes for addressing conflict revolve around Human Resource policies designed to get people to work together. It is often a subset of policies and practices that foster interpersonal relationships in the workplace. The result is that many conflicts don't get resolved.

Allow me to be clear about something before I go further. Several practitioners in this field wrote important books about this subject.

These books contain valuable tools and techniques for advancing successful conflict resolution. I use many of these ideas and tools in my work to help my clients resolve conflicts and not manage them.

Entrenched Faulty Theories

Managing conflict in the context noted above becomes a pretext for managing differences using someone in the company to advocate for different groups. The focus on managing conflict is also given impetus by many of the regulatory requirements that talk about the need to protect the interests of various stakeholders.

Placing the interests of stakeholders before concrete actions take place to resolve the conflict only serves to keep the respective interests intact, making conflict resolution secondary.

Many of us who are called on to assist in resolving conflict find this entrenched idea challenging to overcome because it is an objective built into many company procedures and policies, both explicitly and implicitly. From my perspective, I see this particular idea as a recipe that guarantees conflicts will endure.

How then do we identify criteria that advance the resolution of the conflict? In almost every case, three basic ideas are a crucial part of this process.

1. Defining the criteria necessary for success begins with identifying what is achievable.

   This first component is critical in that those most deeply involved in a conflict will almost always want more than what can reasonably be achieved, so the goal is to determine what is achievable and what is not.

2. Once the desired outcome is understood and agreed to, the parties need to document the pathway(s) to that outcome.

   This is so that all parties involved understand and agree to what is required; especially as to who does what and when.

3. The course of action(s) need to be detailed to evaluate progress so that the parties to the dispute can see measurable progress toward the desired outcome. In parallel, it is necessary to establish that existing policies and procedures both allow and support the actions agreed to and undertaken.

I can't overstate the importance of the alignment between process and action.

It is key to the next part of the criteria process: establishing the decision-makers early, including them in the process, and achieving acceptance of their authority to make decisions.

Following closely after this is: identifying personnel key to a successful outcome and allocating resources to accomplish what is achievable in the conflict-resolution process.

Harmonizing Agreement and Outcome

Achieving what is possible sets the stage for ownership of the outcome by those most closely involved in the conflict to assure the agreement reflects their concerns accurately.

The Point of Convergence: A Path to Understanding Conflict Resolution

This step-by-step process often meets the parties' expectations as to the desired outcome, and, sometimes, the parties achieve more than expected.

By now, those reading this book understand my core conviction: Conflict resolution comes through the execution of a process, and a vital part of that process is understanding how to identify the criteria needed to reach a successful outcome.

1. I begin with a somewhat overused word – clarity – which is a noun. We use Nouns to identify something. So what do you want to determine to start the conflict resolution process?

    (a) The goal is to find the alternative(s) that support multiple options. Stated differently, the early focus on this first step helps determine the possibilities with the fewest unknowns.

    (b) This, in turn, allows for transparency and the ability of multiple stakeholders to assess the options consistently.

2. The second criterion necessary to the process is to establish the basis for identifying the utility of the alternative(s).

    The question of utility is frequently not given the attention it needs. Often, issues such as practicality, usability, cost, and marketability receive attention late in the process, which can disrupt the momentum.

3.   At this stage, those involved must carefully examine the recommended courses of action to assure that these steps/actions are measurable, and that data (metrics) collected is valid for its intended purpose. Equally important, the measures agreed to operate inside established processes, and do so in a stable manner over time.

Adapt, Integrate and Sustain with Emotional Appeal

When companies examine new ideas, an essential aspect of what they look at is sustainability.

An important test of the durability of the product or process is its adaptability. This question attempts to determine whether the idea is a one-hit-wonder, something with a short shelf life, or something that endures.

In the context of conflict resolution, the question of adaptability seeks to answer similar concerns. If the answer is positive, it creates confidence that the process is adaptable over time, and gives greater certainty that its use in the current conflict is correct.

The criteria for a particular conflict-resolution process comes together by the correct use of two final ideas - integration and adhesion. I began this chapter by using a building foundation analogy to set the stage for what I discuss in this chapter.

That foundation will not work unless it becomes a seamless part of the project or process.

The Point of Convergence: A Path to Understanding Conflict Resolution

Any conflict resolution strategy and its associated process will only work if it fits within the broader organizational strategy. A proposed solution may appear to be a great idea, but if senior management does not see the proposed alternative as fitting into the broader goals of the organization, it won't go anywhere.

A solution, idea, and usable prototype must be "integratable" into the broader whole, or the idea can't be sustained, and this leads to a close corollary I refer to as adhesion. How many times have you heard someone stay, "let's throw it at the board and see if it sticks?

Inside this trite expression lies a vital truth critical to a successful conflict- resolution process. Does the idea have the ability to "stick," can it become an accepted solution? Does it lead to acceptable behavior? Does it have an emotional appeal?

These are essential questions, and the last is particularly important because it goes to the heart of acceptance by the parties in dispute. The most desired outcome to a conflict is a way forward that both sides can accept, feel satisfied with, and adopt with confidence.

Ultimately, none of it happens unless the idea, or solution, has emotional appeal. If it does, it will stick, and others will see this as a way forward.

One final caveat on criteria. Solutions to conflict always carry the obligation to assess the cost/benefit consequences. Companies are not charities, nor are their actions altruistic.

They have an obligation to pursue outcomes that do not adversely impact their ability to make a profit.
Consequently, solutions to any particular conflict are required to meet the profitability test.

To some, this may seem overly cynical, but make no mistake about this. Any solution to a conflict that puts an organization under financial stress, whether it be a company or a department within a company, will very quickly abandon that solution, and the parties to the conflict will have to start over.

Chapter 9

Dispute versus Conflict

We are masters of the unsaid words, but slaves of those we let slip out. (Winston Churchill)

Is it dispute, or is it conflict? Is this a chicken-versus-egg argument, or a distinction that matters? In my more cynical moments, I call them twins separated at birth.

To stay both current and historically informed in my work, I spend time reading material from many different sources. This chore is made easier by the fact that I like to read. Recently, my literary perusals led me to a book involving industrial relation disputes in the early part of the 20th century. This era of the labor movement was decidedly non-peaceful. It was, in fact, the opposite, often violent, bloody, and sometimes deadly.

So it was with some interest that I read about a little known strike involving the Arizona copper mines shortly after the start of World War I. More than 5,000 mine workers struck over inadequate pay and other grievances.

What proved noteworthy about this particular strike is that it was remarkably free of violence. Negotiations were conducted peacefully, and the negotiated dispute led to labor harmony for a good number of years after the strike was settled.

That the event was essentially peaceful from start to finish is why it never made it into the history books or became a case study in some dry-as-dirt college textbook.

The part that interested me most was what the writer said about the financial impact of the strike. The impact of the strike, in terms of lost wages on the part of the workers, and the revenue those companies lost is an issue that many ignore. It is noteworthy that neither side ever recovered their losses, even though workers after that made a higher wage, and the companies saw good profits in the years following the strike.

Fast forward 100 years and similar situations confront us daily. They may not involve labor disputes per se, but the basic fact remains – conflict exacts a cost, and the price can be high. Businesses of all sizes face a whole range of issues that apply to many industries, as well as other issues that affect particular sectors.

Regardless of the industry involved or the size of the business, however, conflicts impact a company's financial health, its organizational performance, its culture, employee morale, and the resources that a company allocates to achieve its objectives.

When one sifts through the debris that conflict leaves in its wake, it is often cultural issues that lie at the heart, and which damage a company's efforts to do its work.

The Power of Cultural Difference

Let your sympathies and your compassion be always with the underdog in the fight – this is magnanimity; but bet on the other one – for this is business. (Mark Twain)

Disputes whose components are primarily cultural are not well understood, not discussed early or adequately, and addressed through a variety of temporary fixes that only alleviate the problem in the short term. I will touch on this further in the last chapter.

People are learning that culture is a powerful force. It defines how a company or organization sees itself, and it shapes how it presents itself, its products, and services. A company's culture develops from its policies, procedures, regulations, and rules; which is why conflicts rooted in cultural disputes have such a strong impact.

Modern culture's impact on the business environment isn't always positive, and many aspects of our culture have a negative effect that isn't always recognized or understood. One of those negative impacts is the loss of language discipline. Any of us can point to several reasons why people in the workforce today do not practice language discipline, and many of us can find examples.

Resolving conflict in the workplace is challenging enough for people who have some training and skill, but it becomes an impossible challenge for the unskilled because the language surrounding workplace conflicts leads us down unclear paths.

101

The Point of Convergence: A Path to Understanding Conflict Resolution

For an average employee, the words *disagreement, argument, conflict*, and *dispute* are considered synonymous. When we focus and listen to conversations in the workplace, we'll hear employees use these words within the same narrow spectrum, giving little attention to their differences.

To illustrate the point, let's look at two of these words – dispute, and conflict. Here in the U.S., a person or a company has two ways to pursue a grievance; the first and most familiar is through litigation.

The right to petition a court to hear our complaint is a foundational pillar in our constitution, and it reflects a right going back almost 800 years. Litigation (the right to seek justice in a courtroom) is taught to students as early as middle school (or at least it used to be).

Early Conflict, Final Dispute

Once a person or a company hires an attorney, the legal system sees this as a dispute between two parties. Disputes are not treated the same as a conflict for a very good reason. Look around, and you will see a thousand conflicts, and the vast majority will be small. You see them at work, at church, at home, while driving, while shopping, working out at the gym, and in many other places.

Most will be resolved organically, and usually on the spot. Only a few conflicts fail to resolve themselves, escalating instead to a need for third-party intervention. While I've touched on this point already, it deserves further scrutiny.

Because some disputes do not lend themselves to resolution through the legal system, an alternative method developed some 40 years ago, the use of which has grown dramatically in the last 20 years. This method, called Alternative Dispute Resolution, contains several approaches, including arbitration, assorted forms of mediation, conflict coaching, and facilitation.

A judge resolves disputes that follow the "litigation track," sometimes with a jury, sometimes not. It is the court then that decides who wins and who loses. Arbitration, while following more relaxed processes, is essentially the same thing; a third-party neutral individual decides who is right or wrong, and apportions liability accordingly.

As a practical matter, the workplace does not see a dispute in its legal context. For most employees, the legal distinctions don't come into play, at least not right away, and maybe not for some time.

To them, a dispute and a conflict are the same because they are in an environment where suspicion, lack of trust, and some degree of fear define their responses. For those reading this, the differences between the two are this. Conflict is a dynamic state, and a dispute is a process.

In a business environment where a disruptive conflict is creating havoc, it is the dynamic that matters. The legal niceties, while important, don't matter until it gets bumped upstairs. At this point, it is no longer two or more people not able to resolve something. Once it moves up the chain of command, it's no longer minor.

Anytime those higher in the chain of command get involved, a simple conflict, a small disagreement changes into a dispute. Senior management must now decide how to proceed and what role the players have, if any, in mapping out a resolution. The language that becomes important is the language management uses in what is now a process.

Previously I discussed the catalyst and a catapult, a factor that escalates a disagreement into something more. When does a disagreement stop being a difference of opinion? When something new is introduced. That new thing that changes the dynamic is the Argument. Once a disagreement moves into the argument stage, instability increases – sometimes rapidly. It is that transition from disagreement to an argument that exposes the flaws in a given work environment, and involvement by others becomes unavoidable.

The interesting thing about the argument stage is that it can come before the conflict stage or after.

When the arguments crystalize early, it sometimes acts to limit conflict and is one of the reasons people try to find workarounds; because they know that two people arguing will result in no one agreeing to anything.

Once the parties become hostile to the other party's point of view, which is the point where suspicion and distrust have taken over, the re-injection of the arguments is often the spark or catalyst that causes the final break between the parties and the conflict begins to impact other departments.

In my work, I use the following diagram to illustrate the typical sequence from disagreement to dispute. It is important to emphasize that it is simply one way of looking at the issues.

DISAGREEMENT → ARGUMENT → CONFLICT → DISPUTE

In Chapter 3, I introduced the idea of disagreement and why people are reluctant to deal with it. Resolving a difference requires consensus, and when done correctly, building consensus is time-consuming. I've come to believe that a company's leadership demonstrates a significant failure when they don't train employees to resolve disagreements through a consensus process.

Leaders should make clear, but often don't, that building consensus is the point in interpersonal relationships where the power to succeed early lies in the employees' hands, and employees should feel free to do this.

There's no getting around the fact that time, in a work environment, is a scarce commodity, and it is a brave employee who suggests to his/her supervisor that more time is needed. Not only is time always an issue, but building consensus requires the employees most involved to take a risk in getting to a solution, an action many are reluctant to take.

The words argument, conflict, and dispute all have one thing in common: compromise. As stated earlier in this chapter, many in the workplace use words interchangeably, and do so to their detriment. These three in particular, do have one thing in common, but they reflect dramatically different conditions and environments.

Once the parties involved in a disagreement allow it to escalate beyond the point where consensus is still possible, the situation changes. Beyond this point, compromise in the only outcome available.

At the argument stage, achieving a compromise rests with those most closely involved, but more often than not, they don't take advantage of the opportunity because the window of opportunity is narrow. By this time, the supervisor is asking unpleasant questions as to why things are taking so long, and those involved in the argument begin playing defense.

In Chapter 7, I wrote about the consequences to employees' careers when an argument transitions to a dispute. I want to conclude this chapter with a brief explanation of why the idea of conflict in the workplace has two aspects. As noted above, conflicts occur all the time, and most resolve themselves in real-time and organically.

Around five percent do not resolve themselves organically at the place and time they occur, and the real purpose for this book is to map solutions for that five percent.

This small percentage of conflicts is the source of great harm that few companies recognize in time to prevent or mitigate escalation.

Across a broad spectrum of the business world, company procedures and processes don't function in ways that identify that small number of conflicts early enough to understand their outsized impact on the organization. Many companies, fortunately, are starting to understand this and are looking at what they can do to change this dynamic, but it is early days yet, and they have a long way to go.

This small percentage of destructive conflicts is what my company focuses on, and the clients we serve come to us to help identify where within the organization, those conflicts may be percolating out of sight.

The Point of Convergence process is an integral part of our company's core services, and one purpose of this book is to draw more leaders and business owners to look at conflict with a finer magnifying tool.

When/How to Introduce the Why

Earlier in the book, I reviewed the four "W's" – What, When, Where, and Who. At that point, I emphasized that the Why question was a question best left for later, and I outlined the reason - introducing it too soon would cause more harm than good.

The "why" has value in only two places.

1. One is in the lessons-learned phase when a company's leadership is looking to take corrective action or make improvements in relevant procedures and processes.

2. The second is when a formerly hidden conflict is uncovered. The recognition of a hidden conflict with the potential to cause significant harm will drive two key questions,

   a. How did it remain below the surface for as long as it has?

   b. And why?

An analysis of what these two questions reveal frequently discloses motives and behaviors that are at odds with a company's core values and standards.

Once a hidden conflict is exposed, these questions will show, more often than not, that the motives and behaviors belong to employees who fill important roles in that company. Sometimes the incompatible motivations and actions emanate from the C-suite, but what is more common is for employees with separate agendas to operate between the C-suite and the supervisor.

One other point about the Why question: Even the most skilled senior executives don't handle it well.

Most businesses operate on a hierarchical structure that makes it inevitable that leaders – even those skilled at asking questions – will inject a prosecutorial tone to the pursuit of an answer.

Not only does an organization's structure drive the use of this question, but outside influences also play a role. The "Why" is a subtext in much of what goes on behind what we recognize as conflict.

In the remaining two chapters, I will examine the role outside influences play in creating and hiding the motives and behaviors that often are at odds with a company's standards and values.

I place them at the back the book because I challenge traditional thinking on these issues, which can impact much more than the small percentage of conflicts mentioned in this chapter that escalate to a level of dispute. I readily admit that we'll be concentrating now on conflicts of the lower-level 95 percent.

However, my purpose is to demonstrate that these outside forces have an outsized influence on the five percent of conflicts that require senior management attention.

Chapter 10

Right and Wrong

".....What then is the foundation for the rules an individual lives by or that a company uses to establish its code of conduct? Simply stated, the principles one defines for himself, or a company defines for itself, become the foundation." (Jerry Cooper)

I created a provocative title for this chapter with a specific purpose in mind. Some of our strongest rules, our greatest obligations, and the most impacting of actions we demand of ourselves are stated as a negative.

They are among the earliest obligations we learn as we mature, such as "don't lie, don't steal," and "don't harm others," are stated in the negative.

In reality, such commitments are not negatives but perceived as such. A company's Code of Conduct first lists the "do not do this or that" directives, and only when those are described, does the codes of conduct identify positive standards. Negativity does exist in all companies, and it surrounds employees.

All of us experience such comments as "the report's late, we are behind schedule," and "tell me why this or that happened." The environment management allows to exist defines the type of feedback employees receive. As I approach the end of this book, our nation is in the midst of an event of historic proportions.

We are engaged in a national exercise of self-quarantine in response to a deadly virus with the capability to harm a great many of us. Before this event, the corporate landscape contained every human dynamic possible. Many of those dynamics exerted powerful negative influences on work environments, large and small.

With my clients, and when speaking to business groups here in Houston, I make a point of talking about the high number of employees who disengaged from their jobs on a weekly or daily basis. Studies show those numbers can exceed 45% of a company's workforce during any given week.

Most senior leaders running these companies are aware of this problem. They spend a lot of money on programs aimed at re-engaging the employees with the company and the work they do. The data indicates the initiatives have yielded mixed success.

The workplace environments all of us are familiar with are gone. What comes after is unclear, and this uncertainty dominates much of our conversation. What is not uncertain is that human interaction will continue to drive conflict. Our Point of Convergence methodology places us in a unique position to understand and react to these changes as they evolve.

Negative Influences Trickle Both Ways

CEO's and other senior leaders may argue otherwise, but it is the negatives that dominate many of the environments inside many companies. From the supervisor upward, many of those behaviors are tacitly allowed to go unchecked. They drive fault-finding, mistakes, excuses, the blame game, and any number of other actions that are detrimental to the employee and the company.

My most recent book focused on behaviors that strengthen the ethical culture of a company and those that damage a company in significant ways. This book focuses on the behaviors that drive conflict and those that impede the timely resolution of a whole range of disagreements.

The title of this chapter, Right and Wrong, is not about moral foundations. I wrote about that in my "Battle" book, and it is a subject that I believe does not get the attention it deserves inside the corporate environment. I've heard the arguments against introducing the topic of moral foundations into a corporate setting, and I don't think those arguments hold up well in logical and rational discussions.

I will briefly state what I've written about before. Everything begins with integrity—everything from human interactions to the integrity of physical objects. If you are an engineer or work in the technology field, you understand that incorporating triangles into a design can significantly strengthen a structure in many ways.

Conversely, when you fail to factor triangles into a plan, you limit the use of that structure in significant ways. I operate from the firm conviction that the concept of a triangle is also key to successful conflict resolution.

Everyone in business works or has worked in a company with its list of do's and don'ts. Everyone also knows that in their company's Code of Conduct, the don'ts appear first, followed by the important do's. In the same way these codes place the don'ts first, so must you put the same importance on the don'ts when it comes to understanding the unraveling of a conflict.

One trademark platform of my methodology is the Conflict Triangle, and we use it to identify things that are "not supposed to happen," but were allowed to happen, regardless. Using this process, we can unravel the wrong actions, and then connect them to subsequent negatives. It's called, "Understanding the wrong thing done for the wrong reason at the wrong time."

Our proprietary process converts this triangle into a conflict-resolution process that refocuses a person's attention toward considering the "don'ts" that almost always start with that first disagreement.

The process coaches/trains key individuals to perceive the opposite of the negative through our Doing the Right Thing at the Right Time for the Right Reason® methodology. It is the foundation of our Conflict Triangle – and what we call our conflict-resolution process.

Applying the Leadership Role Responsibly

The whole purpose of looking at conflict in these terms is to expose a critical failure for which senior leaders must take responsibility. Almost no one talks about the characteristics of conflict. Everyone can name at least five sources of conflict in an organization; yet, ask anyone about the *characteristics* typical to workplace conflicts, and virtually no one answers the question correctly.

Forgive me for repeating myself, but conflict is a natural consequence of human interaction, and for most of us it is not a comfortable experience initially. People learn, however, and respond to most conflicts as they are supposed to – constructively. Why? Because conflicts arise in the normal course of uncovering differences and are usually resolved organically.

A broad category of conflicts arises when a natural difference of opinion attaches itself to an important issue. The uncertain issue might be as common as a key element of the work to be done, individual work schedules, or other concerns that employees need to act in concert to achieve an objective.

It is here, within this category, that disagreement is created, and here that the organic resolution of conflict no longer functions. Failure or success depends on whether those employees immediately involved in the controversy understand the next step, and, equally crucial, whether their immediate supervisor/manager understands that next step.

Many companies now recognize that resolving things early by consensus-building is key to preventing or mitigating conflicts. I sense, however, that a majority of companies still miss this

114

critical concept. The key reason is that senior leaders either miss or dismiss the starting point for building consensus.

A Closer Look at the Gap

What created the issue that created the disagreement? As noted earlier, more than a few senior leaders fail to take responsibility for the gap between expectation and execution. That's unfortunate because this gap does not occur just once.

The gap between expectation and execution shows up repeatedly at several points in an organization, and this gap is the genesis for the issue, or issues, over which disagreements develop. Nearly everyone I've spoken to on this subject in the past year has an opinion on what constitutes consensus. Upon discussion, more than half – 50 to 60 – percent got to the heart of the issue quickly and understood what I was asking.

Recognizing that this was an anecdotal process, I came out of these discussions concluding more than 40 percent of those I spoke with use the terms consensus and compromise interchangeably; to them, the two words meant essentially the same thing.

I found that those who fell into the second category had a negative view of both words.

For many of them, the word "compromise" was seen as particularly negative, and because they see the two terms as interchangeable, both have negative connotations.

The Key to Compromise is Mutual Give-and-Take

The meaning of compromise has been poisoned to some degree by certain aspects of our popular culture, and I will address cultural ramifications in more detail in the next chapter. Those who misunderstand the correct use of either word, misunderstand what compromise entails. They see compromise as a failure, although the opposite is the case.

When asked a different but related question, their attitude dramatically underscored their confusion about compromise. Among those in the smaller group, I asked if they saw "agreement" as the primary goal of negotiation. Almost to a person, they answered in the affirmative, that the purpose of negotiation was to reach an agreement.

When I explained that the definition of compromise was to reach an agreement, they struggled to get past their perception of negativity associated with the word. Once they worked through that, the all-important difference between consensus and compromise finally became clear.

To compromise means to balance the give-and-take. Both factions must consider "what's in it for me?" and "what's in it for them?" The willingness to drill down to the basics allows a successful compromise.

Let's say the produce market is running low on produce, and only three apples remain in the bin. A man and woman reach for them at the same time. She has promised to bake a pie for a benefit luncheon.

116

He needs to make lunches for his three children, and one of them is particularly picky. In his basket, he already has the last two unblemished bananas. He needs one of those apples, but she can't make a pie with only two.

After a conversation, with both people willing to give-and-take, he phones his wife for her prized cranberry-apple pie recipe, which is always a show-stealer, and only requires two apples. Fortunately, the market still has plenty of cranberries.

A business person reading the above example will likely shake his/her head and say to himself, "that's not a realistic example," but if you've spent any time at a farmer's market, that kind of give and take does take place. Once again, context matters.

The Key to Consensus is Optimistic Alliance

The Oxford English definition of consensus is elegantly simple: an opinion or conclusion that all members of a group agree with. It is a word that requires no lengthy definition, nor does it require multiple interpretations.

Where it gets interesting – and challenging – is in the techniques used to achieve consensus. Building consensus requires dialogue, which brings us back to the title of this chapter, Right and Wrong.

As most of us know, or should know, a group with conflicting opinions and needs cannot simply jump into a dialogue. Any discussion toward consensus must be prefaced by a solid foundation, and again I apologize for being a bit repetitive.

The Point of Convergence: A Path to Understanding Conflict Resolution

So what does a solid foundation for dialogue look like? Building consensus successfully has a subtle but powerful key. It's not an obvious key, like the key to a door or box. If you don't find the key, you won't achieve a successful outcome in your efforts to build consensus.

The meaning of success in consensus is that everyone agrees. Note, however, that getting everyone to *accept* a course of action is not the same as to *agree*, and will lead to conflict later. It is important in building consensus that the differences between agreement and acceptance be openly discussed and understood.

Everyone involved in a given conflict-resolution process needs to be comfortable moving toward a solution, or set of solutions, on which everyone can agree. Motives and agendas need to be gently excavated and put to rest. This requires courage. It requires time. Above all, it requires the unwavering support of the leader empowered to ultimately approve the outcome.

An important caveat exists. Getting to an agreement means discarding those things which cannot reasonably be achieved – because of budget or scheduling issues, or because the company's senior leadership will not support certain options.

Getting to consensus is a process of reduction. This reduction process is a cooperative process through which competing objectives are distilled through a collaborative dialogue. Members of the group must agree to operate in good faith.

The Point of Convergence: A Path to Understanding Conflict Resolution

This is an essential starting point. As any mediator will tell you, the process will work only if the parties are willing to use it fairly and impartially to achieve a settlement agreement with which they can live. Mediations fail when the parties do not want or are unwilling to find alternative solutions.

Once good faith is established, the process requires all group members working in concert to seek the two best alternatives to be examined. Why two alternatives?

Allow me to be blunt, the goal is not unanimity, for that is the road to failure. The goal is a single course of action, which may require several steps to attain.
Getting to a single course of action requires:

1. All members of the group have to agree – at the beginning – that their preference may not survive.

2. The next step is to create a positive discussion environment that a) encourages trust and good faith. The process works when everyone wants a positive outcome, and b) the parties give respectful attention to every individual's ideas and opinions.

3. Next, start a winnowing process to remove everything least attractive to most individuals until the alternatives narrow down to two possibilities that receive everyone's approval.

4. The group commits to work through these; ultimately choosing one they all agree to support.

It is not about any individual preference. Achieving consensus is both a process and a goal. An integral part of a consensus process is the recognition that members of the group act in concert with one another and want the process to succeed. Efforts to achieve consensus often fail because:

1. The actions of one or more members to force the other members of the group to act collectively,

2. By error or by design, vote-casting begins before the choices have been reduced to two equally agreeable alternatives.

Forcing the group into collectively addressing issues will lead to acceptance, not agreement. Equally important, a group operating collectively will not arrive at only two alternatives for open discussion until one is ultimately selected. Collective action will result in more than two choices, which will force the group dynamic to cast votes.

The alternative receiving the most votes being the one unhappily acted upon, and this will not solve the conflict; only push it back beneath the surface.

Most groups operating collectively never get that far because, once those controlling the choices move toward their preferred options, good faith goes out the window. The group breaks down, and the process goes back to square one.

Please do not misunderstand; in a group acting *in concert*, the members choose one of two alternatives, but at that point, it is a contest between two *acceptable* approaches. When that vote comes to the table, it stands on a foundation of good faith.

Actions taken in a collective decision-making process are antithetical to the goals of consensus building.

Many of the failures in the conflict-resolution arena can be traced to the injection of top-down decision making, either too soon, or out of a lack of confidence in the process.

Chapter 11

The Cultural Paradox

There is nothing more difficult to take in hand, more perilous to conduct, or more uncertain in its success, than to take the lead in the introduction of a new order of things. (Nicolo Machiavelli)

At several points in this book, I take a piece of history to provide context for what I want to say. Arriving now at this juncture in your reading, you've also come across brief commentaries on the dangers and pressures of conducting business in our broad-American culture.

A casual appraisal of this book might lead one to believe I have an unfavorable view of the culture I was born into and reared. That would be a false conclusion.

At the risk of being a bit jingoistic, I would not live anywhere else. Very few, if any, other cultures compare favorably to ours for many reasons, and most of us would benefit greatly by engaging in thoughtful conversations about why our culture is so unique.

Having lived more than 20 years of my life outside the United States, I experienced other cultures first-hand, and wherever I went, the limitations were stark. The comparisons between our culture and most others fall apart very quickly.

That said, some of the things that are good for us in our overall culture are not desirable inside a company, and not for

122

the reasons you might initially think. Companies do not operate on democratic principles, nor should we expect them to.

When individuals undertake any venture, they have a societal obligation to do no harm and to obey the law, but beyond that, they are accountable only to themselves.

In contrast, companies are accountable to multiple entities and individuals for how they conduct their business, and for how their employees conduct themselves. Moreover, companies are not charitable endeavors; they succeed when they make a profit, and disappear when they don't.

These brief examples are but two of many I might have chosen to demonstrate that what works for an individual does not work inside a company. Conversely, many things about our culture that are good and positive are also necessary for a company to operate successfully.

In significant ways, American companies are a reflection of the American culture and generally speaking, that is a good thing.

Our culture is rooted in the unique convergence of history and geography that led to the creation of a nation separated from most countries of that era by the two great oceans.

This unique convergence of time, geography, and migration produced a culture under which our country has flourished for nearly 250 years.

Yet, in any culture, and that includes ours, people co-exist in ways that can create tension. Tensions play out in a great many dramas every year. Some of those dramas lead to great change, and we experience such changes every few generations, including the one we are living through now.

Other tensions have their origins in one of the less desirable aspects of our culture, creating conflicts that may lead to severe problems, if not resolved. You and I often hear or read statements that clash with what we understand as the right way to act or speak.

Such statements may not stop with people offering a different opinion but go beyond that to criticizing those who disagree with them. This is only one manifestation of what we now call Political Correctness, and whenever I hear that term, I have to lecture myself not to over-react.

Those who respond to something said or written, and scathingly call it Political Correctness, are saying, "They" need to stop it. Contemptuous complainers take the attitude that someone has to do something – just not the person complaining.

Indicting something as being PC, misses the heart of the issue.
What most of us react negatively to, and call PC, is propaganda, which is far more unwholesome than many realize.

Simply stated, propaganda is information, ideas, or statements that may be intentionally false, or may present

124

only one side of an argument used to gain support for a political leader, party, or any special-interest group.

The spreading of propaganda is a technique condemned for most of the last century because it was used by tyrannical governments to control the people residing in those countries.

In some cases, similar misinformation was then used to intimidate countries these tyrannies wanted to control. Propaganda also was a key method of deliberate misdirection and false communication in World War II, then throughout much of the Cold War with the Soviet Union and other countries sympathetic to communism.

It remains today a tool of misdirection used in this country by a wide number of special interest groups. Many of these groups work hard at making what they do sound legitimate, without any regard for the long term harm they cause.

Back to Our Subject at Hand

How does any of this relate to conflict resolution in business? Here is a simple truth: the majority of conflicts occur because of how people use words, and the actions those words generate.

It should surprise no one reading this that conflict can quickly arise when someone says the wrong thing, at the wrong time, in the wrong place, to the wrong person.

Human conflict has been around for as long as humans have walked the earth, and the words that help resolve conflict have been around for almost as long. What happens to conflict resolution when the meaning of words are changed, and their usefulness in resolving conflict goes away?

If traditional words are replaced with other, more effective, words that express the same meaning, none would see this as an issue. When meant for resolving conflicts, however, that is not the case. What I have discovered is that words central to conflict-resolution are being replaced or watered down.

It's happening for two reasons. One reason can best be described by quoting the author William Souder, who writes, *"... I am constantly reminded that our shared understanding of "ordinary" words isn't what it used to be. Everyday language is increasingly an approximation of proper English".*

"...People misuse words ever more frequently, confusing assumed meanings with original meanings, and picking up habits of speech only because certain mistakes have become so common that everyone now understands them to mean what they did not mean in the first place".

Mr. Souder goes on to say that he understands, as most of us do, that living languages evolve.

English is no different from other languages in that regard. Yet, there is a cost and a danger when changes do not grow organically.

In his article, Souder recognizes that many of the changes in how words are used results from ignorance. In the normal evolution of language, common usage changes because of

126

generational developments, with young people introducing new versions of slang; or it can happen through advances occurring in industry, in communication methods, and where technology changes introduce new words.

In the normal evolution of language, common usage changes or simply becomes correct usage. Mr. Souder further states that what is going on now is not evolution, but the result of English being spoken by people who've never been taught correctly.

The rapid expansion in our population over the past 50 years is creating unforeseen consequences. Large numbers of people who each speak a first language that is not English have adversely impacted how English is now taught in this country.
I have read data that places the number of people living in the U.S., whose first language is not English, at greater than 26%.

What is occurring is an evolution of language, driven by misunderstanding or ignorance, leading to situations where words and phrases are used differently from their original meaning.

This separation of words from the definition most of us assume is correct creates barriers that make communicating with others more difficult than it should be.

The breakdown of distinctive meaning and context creates the risk of a less robust language, making it more difficult to say what we mean, especially when it is essential to do so.

The second reason is that important words are replaced by different words, or their original definitions are deliberately changed, and the motives for this are not so innocent. The deliberate corrupting of a word's meaning is one of the less desirable aspects of our modern culture.

The orchestrated attack on language is not a tin hat conspiracy. Others have written about how and why words are being forced to fit new meanings.

Some of these changes may appear benign at first glance. Yet, even small changes have a significant impact. For example, replacing the phrase "goodwill" with the word "civility" may seem like a good thing. Civility is a word that sounds more erudite and implies a desirable state for negotiating.

Take a closer look, though, and you understand that civility is about promoting social harmony – harmony within a group. When civility is practiced in place of goodwill, protecting the purpose or dynamic of the group takes precedence over resolving the conflict.

If the group's purpose is hampered or affected by options and actions necessary to resolve a conflict, those options/actions may not be accepted.

It often results in the de facto managing of a conflict over resolving it. Goodwill is the basis for good faith, and it is through good faith that conflict is resolved. The same is happening with another word critical to resolving disputes, and that is "compromise." The classical meaning of this word was: to compromise means to reach an agreement.

The Oxford English dictionary still maintains this classical meaning, but Merriam-Webster's definition gives the word a strong negative connotation: "...the making or giving of concessions."

Again, to the uninitiated, this change may not seem all that significant, but its new meaning creates a real barrier to overcoming conflict. This change in the definition and tone of the word is relatively recent.

The 1995 edition of Webster aligned with the Oxford Dictionary, but in 2005, they no longer aligned. What caused this change? Various special interest groups in this country are waging a propaganda campaign against traditional concepts and ideas.

One of their more recognizable goals is disharmony. Their stated goal is to promote conflict while pursuing an ultimate objective, and one technique for achieving this is to change how we use important words.

A growing awareness of the increased frequency of conflicts is bringing much-needed attention to finding better methods for dealing with issues before they get out of control.

Fortunately, the business world is awakened to the fact that a major contributor to conflict in the workplace is the failure to adjust to the impact of today's broader cultural issues and how companies approach interpersonal relationships.

Accommodating religious differences is an area that most companies addressed some years ago. Unfortunately, having done that, a lot of companies felt the job was complete.

If they were lucky, they learned the short-sighted nature of that perception early rather than later.

Unfortunately, many companies remain tone-deaf to such lessons. They fail to fully recognize that companies in America employ people from all over the world whose understanding of English is not the same as that of someone born in this country and raised with the language in "its natural habitat."

Those born and reared here have at their command a vast array of vernacular and colloquialisms that allow them to maneuver through the spoken language with far less effort than someone who grew up elsewhere.

In that separation between those born into the language, and those who were not is where many workplace conflicts develop.

" The paradox of the human condition is expressed more in education than elsewhere in human culture, because learning to learn has been and continues to be Homo Sapiens' most formidable evolutionary task...

It must also be clear that we will never quite learn how to learn, for Homo Sapien is self-changing, and since the more culture changes the faster it changes, and man's methods and rate of learning will never keep pace with his need to learn. (Jules Henry)

This book is about the Points of Convergence inside companies where behaviors create negative downstream consequences. At various places in these chapters, I offered my perspective on the nature and character of these breakpoints.

Unless you are trained to do so, it is hard to see these events in real-time. Each point of convergence widens the gap between expectation and execution because leaders and managers make decisions in-the-moment.

Leaders and managers perceive them to be the right decisions, but a decision made in-the-moment may contain critical flaws.

My goal in writing this book is to shine a light on long-standing perceptions and suggest that new conversations are warranted and overdue.

I thank those of you who've read this book and want you to know I appreciate the great courtesy you demonstrated by buying this book and giving it your time.

ABOUT THE AUTHOR

Jerry Cooper is the founder, CEO, and President of Cooper, Druesne, and Cooper (CDC Integrated Services, LLC). He is a student of conflict and the behaviors that drive conflict in the corporate world.

This book is the product of almost 40 years as a leader, manager, consultant, negotiator, mediator, coach, and business owner. He brings to this book a range of unique experiences that formed the foundation for the work he does.

He was born in the mountains of eastern Arizona when that area was one of the major Copper producing areas of the country. Of English and Scottish descent, Mr. Cooper is the son of a 10th generation miner and can trace his family back to even earlier than 16th century England.

Although born in Arizona, because of his father's work, Mr. Cooper, his brothers and sister, grew up in small mining towns along the spine of Mexico's Sierra Madre Mountains.

As a boy growing up in Mexico, he came in contact with farmers, ranchers, Indians such as the Yaqui and the Tarahumara, and learned to hunt and fish at a young age.

He learned about his family's history and migration to America before the Revolutionary War, and their westward migration to the iron ore and copper mining areas in the Michigan Upper Peninsula in the early 1840s.

132

He grew up in an environment that did not include television. His family had a radio, a large collection of records, and many books.

His father James, a survivor of German POW camps, witnessed much death and destruction and gave his son one piece of advice, "...choose work where things get built. Don't chase money, build your own path, but always work toward making things better."

Jerry Cooper chose to work in what we now call the energy sector, with a near-constant focus on the building of things. Beginning with a power plant in his home state of Arizona, then a pipeline in Alaska, and on to nuclear power plants in California and Washington, then pipelines and platforms in Mexico and Venezuela, and refinery expansions in Texas.

He took what he learned and started his own company. From all of these experiences came the core ideas framed within the covers of this book.

He and his wife Corinne, their three grown children and three grandsons, all make their home in Houston, Texas.